Francis Raymond Stark

The Abolition of Privateering and the Declaration of Paris

Francis Raymond Stark

The Abolition of Privateering and the Declaration of Paris

ISBN/EAN: 9783337428617

Printed in Europe, USA, Canada, Australia, Japan

Cover: Foto ©Suzi / pixelio.de

More available books at **www.hansebooks.com**

STUDIES IN HISTORY, ECONOMICS AND PUBLIC LAW

EDITED BY THE FACULTY OF POLITICAL SCIENCE OF
COLUMBIA UNIVERSITY
IN THE CITY OF NEW YORK.

Volume VIII] [Number 3

THE ABOLITION OF PRIVATEERING

AND

THE DECLARATION OF PARIS

BY

FRANCIS R. STARK, LL.B., Ph.D.

University Fellow in International Law

COLUMBIA UNIVERSITY

New York

1897

PREFACE

I DESIRE to express my great indebtedness to Professor John Bassett Moore, not only for his kind and courteous advice, but also for placing in my hands a great deal of valuable material with regard to the abolition of privateering, especially some unpublished papers of Mr. Marcy.

F. R. S.

COLUMBIA UNIVERSITY,
February 13, 1897.

CONTENTS

PART I

THE RIGHT OF CAPTURE OF PRIVATE PROPERTY AT SEA

	PAGE
INTRODUCTION	11
CHAPTER I. THE THEORY OF INDIVIDUAL ENMITY	13
CHAPTER II. THE FRENCH SCHOOL	19
CHAPTER III. THE ENGLISH SCHOOL	32
CHAPTER IV. THE ATTITUDE OF THE UNITED STATES	38
SUMMARY	45

PART II

COMPARATIVE SKETCH OF PRIVATEERING BEFORE 1856

CHAPTER I. PRIVATEERING IN ENGLAND	49
1. The Ante-Elizabethan Period	49
2. From the Reign of Elizabeth to the Prize Act of Anne (1708)	60
3. From the Prize Act of Anne to the First Armed Neutrality (1780)	68
4. From the First Armed Neutrality till the Declaration of Paris	78

CHAPTER II. PRIVATEERING IN FRANCE 89
    1. The French Marine before Colbert 89
    2. From Colbert to the Peace of Versailles (1783) . . 94
    3. The Era of Revolution 105

CHAPTER III. PRIVATEERING IN THE UNITED STATES . . . 117
    1. During the Revolution 117
    2. During the War of 1812 127

PART III

THE ABOLITION OF PRIVATEERING

CHAPTER I. THE DECLARATION OF PARIS 139
CHAPTER II. THE WORKING OF THE DECLARATION 153

PART I

THE RIGHT OF CAPTURE OF PRIVATE PROPERTY AT SEA

INTRODUCTION

WHEN the progressive people of a state wish to bring about a reform in their municipal law, their course, however full of obstacles in practice, is theoretically simple. The sovereign, as represented in the supreme legislature of the land, is appealed to, persuaded of the reality of the grievance, and induced to enact a "law" for its abolition. The grievance disappears instantly; and the historian of that people, tracing the fate of that grievance, can lay his hand upon the hour and the minute when it was eradicated from the law.

A reform in the Law of Nations is a very different proceeding. There is no supreme legislature, because there is no sovereign. There is not even a collective sovereignty, so that the majority may bind the minority; for there is no organization in the concert of the nations. The reformer, therefore, since he can find no *one* in authority, must seek the consent of all in turn; and instead of being able to point out the exact instant when the reform is effected, he is able to say only this: that *the greater the number and weight of the states which have adopted it at a given time, the more fully has it become a part of International Law.*

International Law resembles other law in this, that its tendencies are of greater importance than its decisions. It is not what has been decided, but what is likely to be decided next time, that the average litigant is interested to know. And therefore, in estimating the progress of our international reform, we are not confined to the mere enumeration of the states *pro* and *con*. Just as the private lawyer can shrewdly guess which of his book rules are on the verge of being regarded by the courts as "no longer applicable to existing conditions," and obsolete, so the publicist, weighing two theories between which the nations of the earth are divided, is able to decide which is the theory of the future and which is the theory of the past. And if he is writing about the law of the present, he will be influenced more by the former than by the latter.

The right of capture of private property on the high seas in time of war was once universally recognized. At some time in the future, it will not be recognized at all. In order to appreciate the present state of the question as to the existence of this right, it may perhaps be worth while to glance briefly at the two great theories with regard to the nature of war itself, as they developed and as they exist to-day. And first:

CHAPTER I

THE THEORY OF INDIVIDUAL ENMITY

IN the earliest times there was but one theory with regard to the nature of war; the theory that every subject of one belligerent state was the enemy of every subject of the other. There were two reasons, in early times, for assenting to this theory: one itself theoretical, the other practical.

The theoretical reason was this: the conception of the state as distinct from the king or other legal sovereign had not yet developed. The legal sovereign was also the sovereign of political science. War was waged, not by states, but by kings. As it is impossible to conceive a state of war without enemies on either side, and as the idea of the state as a body politic independent of the absolute monarch in whom was concentrated the power of managing its affairs had not yet arisen, it became necessary to regard the absolute monarchs themselves as the primary enemies in every armed conflict; something which was the more easy because in a great many cases the absolute monarchs did, in point of fact, hate each other—*i. e.*, stood to each other in a relation of *actual personal enmity*. Given, however, the theory of enmity between the monarchs, it likewise became necessary, on feudal principles, to consider their subjects enemies; for the great crown vassals in each land held their immense territorial grants of the king on the condition, among others, that they should follow him to war—*i. e.*, make his enemies their own; and their tenants held from them on the same principle, and so on. And thus, when war broke out, every one found himself an enemy of every one upon the other side.

The second and practical reason was that, as wars were in point of fact carried on, the private individuals on each side were always treated as enemies. Military commanders took it for granted that war gave them absolute rights over the persons of all subjects of the foreign prince, and *a fortiori* over all their property, movable and immovable, wherever found; for, as Cicero logically remarks, "It is not improper to despoil the man whom we have the right to kill."[1]

Both of these principles—the absolute right over (1) hostile persons and (2) hostile property—were firmly established in the time of Grotius. Indeed, it would have been folly to have put forward any other theory at that time, with the Thirty Years' War raging and the sack of Magdeburg going on before the almost indifferent eyes of Europe. According to Grotius, a declaration of war against a prince is a declaration against his subjects, who may lawfully (*impune*) be killed wherever found,[2] and whose property is all subject to absolute confiscation.[3] Not only were these principles considered political axioms in Grotius' time, but they were constantly reiterated by writers in the first half of the succeeding century. Wolf states the theory of individual enmity as something unquestionable,[4] and allows the seizure of private property as a consequence, partly to indemnify the captor (*tum ad consequendum debitum*), partly to weaken the resistance of the owner (*tum ad imminuendum vires agendi*).[5] Bynkershoek (1751) lays down the doctrine in its extreme form. It is lawful, says he, to put down the enemy by force.

---

[1] "Non est contra naturam spoliare eum, quem honestum est necare." Quoted by Grotius, *De Jure Belli.ac Pacis*, III., v., 1.

[2] *De Jure Belli ac Pacis*, III., iv., 8.

[3] *Id.*, III., v., 2.

[4] When sovereigns (rectores) declare war, ". . . utriusque subditi sunt invicem hostes." *Jus Gentium*, § 723.

[5] *Ibid.*, § 849.

"I said, by force. Not just force, for all force in war is just; * * * so much so that it is legitimate to destroy the enemy even when unarmed, or by poison or assassination * * *."[1] When he comes to speak of hostile property, we find, of course, that everything is confiscable.[2]

In 1758 M. Emeric Vattel published his *Droit des Gens*. Although in some ways a distinct improvement upon Bynkershoek and even Grotius, he too considered *all the subjects*[3] of two belligerent states mutual enemies, even the women and children,[4] though the latter, being "inoffensive" enemies, should be dealt with gently by Christian armies. With a curious inconsistency, which escaped notice only because Rousseau had not yet written, Vattel gives, as a reason for the theory of individual enmity, the very strongest reason against it: "For the sovereign," says he, "represents the nation, and acts in the name of the whole body politic (*au nom de la société entière*); and nations have nothing to do with one another except collectively, in their quality of nations."

If the sovereign is the representative of the nation, and nothing more; if he acts, not in his own name, but in that of the "*société entière*," it can hardly be correct to say that he individually is an enemy. The agent who does an act on behalf of his principal is not usually, in contemplation of law, a party to the act. It is then the nation which declares war, and "nations have nothing to do with one another except collectively," from which it follows plainly, it would seem, that a declaration of war does not affect the relations between individuals as such at all.

Nevertheless, up to this point the publicists were practically unanimous; and their princes, if possible, even more so. The latter sometimes displayed the greatest ferocity

[1] *Quaestiones Juris Publici*, I., i. [2] *Id.*, III.
[3] *Droit des Gens*, III., v., § 70. [4] *Ibid.*, § 72.

towards the inoffensive subjects of their rivals; and the language of some of the manifestoes of the seventeenth and eighteenth centuries is almost as violent as that of the recent memorable declaration of war by China against Japan. Thus Louis XIV. in his declaration of war against the Dutch in 1672: "* * * His Majesty hath declar'd, as he does now declare, that he has determin'd and resolv'd to make war against the said States-General of the United Provinces, both by Sea and Land; and so consequently commands all his Subjects, Vassals, and Servants to fall upon the *Hollanders*, and forbids them, for the future, to have any Commerce, Communication, or Correspondence with them, upon pain of death."[1] So in 1689, the States-General, in declaring war against France, required all their subjects "to pursue and everywhere in a hostile manner to attack the countrys, people, inhabitants and subjects of the King of *France*,"[2] and the Lieutenant-Governor of the Netherlands issued at Brussels a manifesto in which he exhorted the Spanish troops to "resist the subjects of *France*, to fall upon them, and to commit all Acts of Hostility against them, as against Enemys, Aggressors, and Violators of Treatys."[3]

As yet no hint of any contrary theory is to be found in the proclamation of any prince or the language of any text-writer. But many forces were at work, paving the way for progress in this as in other directions. The belligerent practices were insensibly becoming less savage; and this tendency was being manifested especially in three ways.

[1] *A General Collection of Treatys and other Publick Papers* (London, 1732) I., 167.
[2] *Id.*, I., 260.
[3] *Id.*, I., 272. See also Queen Anne's declaration of 1702, p. 422 (all acts of hostility against *France* and *Spain* or their subjects), and the Emperor's against France and Anjou, 1702, p. 430 (attack our said enemies, and those which belong to them).

First, a well-defined distinction was beginning to be drawn between combatants and non-combatants. The absurdity, as well as the cruelty, of robbing and butchering women and children and harmless peasants was beginning to be apparent even to the imbruted wits of the men who had studied war in the school of Tilly and Wallenstein. When a town fell into the possession of the enemy it was no longer given up to pillage,[1] but a certain sum was raised by the citizens and paid over to the hostile army by way of ransom—a system which soon gave place to the modern one of contributions and requisitions. Secondly, even as to combatants, properly so called, the usage was relaxing. Bynkershoek has been quoted as saying that it is lawful to destroy an enemy even when disarmed;[2] but the spirit of the year 1751, in which Bynkershoek wrote, was far from sanctioning any such general principle. It is difficult to find any satisfactory distinction between the soldier who has thrown away his arms and the peasant who has never taken them up; and as nearly all the nations of the day, Bynkershoek to the contrary notwithstanding, were agreed upon sparing the peasant, it was a natural consequence that the soldier should begin to be spared as well.[3]

A third and important change of usage was that in relation to the treatment of prisoners of war. Formerly, on the feudal theory of personal enmity between belligerents, the body of a prisoner, as well as his property, belonged to the indi-

---

[1] Except, for a long time, the peculiar case of a town defended against overwhelming odds and finally taken by assault. For a criticism of this exception see Hall, *Intern. Law* (1880), 336 n. 3.

[2] *Cf.* supra, *Quaest. Jur. Pub.*, I., I. "Inermem" = either "unarmed" or "disarmed."

[3] Wolf states the principle in his logical, dogmatic way: "Quamprimum hostis in mea potestate est, hostis esse desinit. Hostes enim sunt, inter quos bellum est." *Jus Gentium,* § 795.

vidual who took him.[1] A man might do what he would with *his* enemy, with the captive of *his* bow and spear. Now, however, we find the right of the individual over his prisoner's person, with its accompanying right of ransom, dying out; and substituted for it we find the practice of exchange. The remarkable significance of this transition, in the history of the theory of war, must be obvious, when it is recalled that the exchange of prisoners is a process which does not benefit the individual captor at all, but does benefit the captor's state. What did all this mean but the substitution of the state for the individual as the real party to the war, and the devolution of the individual into the position of a mere agent, to be treated as an enemy only when busy with the state's business?

It was reserved for the French genius—the French republican genius—by simply altering the point of view to suit the growth of political science, to turn a mere bunch of disconnected changes in the practice of war into a revolution in its theory.

[1] Except where the prisoner was a king or other great personage, in which case his ransom went to the captor's sovereign.

CHAPTER II

THE FRENCH SCHOOL

THE changes noted at the close of the last chapter may be ascribed to three concurrent causes: First, humanity; the world was becoming more civilized. Secondly, self-interest—the fear of reprisals and, worse still, disciplinary relaxation. And a third cause underlying both the other two—the development of the conception of the state as a body politic distinct (1) from its ordinary members, and (2) from its legal sovereign.

Given the principle that the state and the king are distinct entities, it follows that states may have relations with one another as states without altering in any respect the relations existing between two or more subjects as individuals. The theoretical reason for the conception of individual enmity in war has entirely disappeared. Even the kings are no longer enemies, but have degenerated into mere officers of the state, mere agents, obnoxious to each other only while acting about the affairs of their principals. There is no longer any legal reason for raising a fictitious enmity between individuals who are not enemies in fact—between parents and children, brothers and sisters, and bosom friends whom there is no magic in a frontier and a declaration of war to separate.[1] Moreover, the old doctrine was objectionable as inhuman

---

[1] "Der Stat ist eine andere Person als die Privatpersonen im State. . . . Daher sind die Privatpersonen nicht im eigentlichen Sinne Feinde. Sie können trotz des Kriegs in den freundlichsten Beziehungen leben, der Verwandtschaft, der Wirthschaft, des Verkehrs." Bluntschli, *Das Moderne Völkerrecht*, § 531 n.

and unchristian. The only ground upon which war was justifiable at all, from a Christian point of view, was that of self-defense; the very etymology of the word depends upon this idea.[1] It is unnecessary to dwell upon the fact that no principle of self-defense can require us to predicate enmity of non-combatants. "The foundation of a just war is a wrong," says Franciscus à Victoria,[2] "but wrong does not proceed from the innocent, therefore it is not lawful to make war upon them." That which was most important of all, however, and which assisted most the decay of the old theory on the Continent, was the change in the practice, which had in fact been so great as fairly to take the kernel out of it and leave little except the bare shell.

Briefly to sum up, if individuals taking no active part in the war were enemies, they were enemies (1) who could not be killed, (2) who could not in any manner be molested in their persons (except in a few cases on the ground of military necessity), and (3) whose property on land was exempt from seizure [3] except by way of contribution and requisition.[4] What, then, was left of the *jus hostilis?*

[1] Calvo, *Droit International* (Paris, 1880), III., 11. "Le mot *guerre* dérive de l'allemand *wehr* . . qui signifie *défense*."

[2] *Relect. Theol.*, VI. Quoted by Hall, *Intern. Law* (Ed., 1880).—"Fundamentum justi belli est injuria, sed injuria non est ab innocente; ergo non licet bello uti contra illum."

[3] If, for example, England and France are at war. and X is a French subject, his personal property on land may be divided into three classes: (1) Property in France; (2) Property in England; (3) Property on land elsewhere. The first class is exempt from seizure except by way of contribution and requisition. The second and third classes are exempt absolutely in practice, though the English writers say, as a sort of sop thrown to consistency, that they are "theoretically subject to seizure." The real property everywhere is exempt, though it may, of course, be occupied by either army during military invasion. The irreconcilability of these exemptions with the old theory that X is the enemy of the English Crown and of every individual Englishman can hardly fail to be apparent.

[4] The right of contribution and requisition is not a hostile right, but depends

Theoretical progress is made in a straight line, but the paths of practical progress are devious. It is not surprising, therefore, that something really was left of the *jus hostilis* in regard to non-combatants. The different methods of warring upon harmless individuals had been falling out of use by degrees, not abolished by one happy stroke; and there was one method which was in use still, for no other reason than that it had not yet been abolished. The capture of private property was still allowed on the high seas. That is to say, if England is at war with Prussia, a bale of Prussian goods is safe on an English wharf, but the same bale found by an English cruiser outside the three-mile line is good and lawful prize. Mably, in 1754, called attention to this unfair discrimination. "We should regard with horror," says he, "an army which made war on citizens and robbed them of their goods; * * * How, I ask, can that which is infamous on land be just or at any rate permissible at sea?"[1]

A few years later Rousseau, in his Social Contract, found the words to express the great principle toward which the laws of war had been tending. "*War*," said he,[2] "*is not at*

upon the principle that the invader displaces, temporarily, the sovereignty of the invaded state over the territory invaded. It is a right analogous to that of the original sovereign to levy war taxes. It is a right exercised by superior over political inferior—not by belligerent over belligerent. *Cf.* Ercole Vidari, *Del rispetto della proprietà privata fra gli Stati in guerra* (Pavia, 1867), III., 3.

Moreover, England now pays for her contributions, and the United States has evinced an intention to do the same. (*Cf. Am. Instr. for the Government of Armies in the Field*, Art. 37, providing for "forced *loans*;" and *Treaty of Guadalupe Hidalgo with Mexico*, 1848, Art. 22.) See also Art. 55 of the Code of the Institute of International Law for wars on land, providing for restitution of things requisitioned.

[1] *Droit Public de l'Europe fondé sur les traités*, II., 310.

[2] "La guerre n' est donc point une relation d'homme à homme, mais une relation d' état à état, dans laquelle les particuliers ne sont ennemis qu' accidentellement; non point comme hommes, ni même comme citoyens, mais comme soldats; non point comme membres de la patrie, mais comme ses défenseurs."— *Du Contrat Social* (1762), I., IV.

all a relation of man to man, but a relation of state to state, in which individuals are enemies only accidentally—not as men, not even as citizens, but as soldiers; not as members of their state, but as its defenders." Principles, he says, which are not those of Grotius, and are not founded on the authority of poets, but which spring from the nature of things and are based on reason.

Obviously the logical result of this theory is the abolition of capture of private property at sea. So clear, indeed, is the connection, that the English claim that it was invented for that purpose.[1] The dilemma was difficult for the supporters of the old system. If non-combatants are enemies, why spare their persons and property on land? If they are not, why interfere with them at sea?

The spread of the new doctrine was very rapid in France. Linguet adopted it in 1779.[2] Portalis substantially quoted Rousseau in his opening speech to the Conseil des Prises on the 14th floréal, an VIII. (1801).[3] From this time on there is a perfect chorus of French writers and diplomatists laying down the Rousseaunian principle as established, and treating the theory of individual enmity as fallen into innocuous desuetude. Vergé, the celebrated annotator of Martens, says that "for a long time" (*longtemps*) war was waged between individual and individual, but that to-day states only are enemies, and consequently private property at sea is no longer justly subject to capture.[4] Talleyrand, writing to Napoleon in 1806, declared that, "in consequence of the principle that war is not a relation of man to man, but of state to state, * * * the law of nations does not permit the right of war

[1] Hall, *Intern. Law* (1880), pp. 60, 61.
[2] *Annales Politiques*, V., 506, quoted by Laveleye, *Rev. de Dr. Intern.*, VII (1875), 560.
[3] Quoted *Ibid.*
[4] Vergé, note to Martens, § 289.

and the resulting right of conquest to extend * * * to
private property, to merchandises of commerce, * * * in a
word, to private persons and their goods."[1] Napoleon himself expressed an ardent wish for the coming of a time "when
the same liberal ideas should be extended" to both maritime
war and terrestrial, and when private merchant vessels and
harmless sailors should no longer be subject to capture.[2]
Cauchy, writing after the Declaration of Paris, and holding
the same views, for the same reasons as his predecessors,
dilates with perhaps a shade too much optimism on the step
taken toward their realization by the abandonment of privateering.[3] In the same breath with the French writers may
be mentioned the celebrated Argentine publicist Calvo,
who writes in French as well as in Spanish, and who says
positively that "war exists between states, and not between
individuals,"[4] and that as a consequence the practice of capturing private property, even at sea, "*tends* to-day to give
way to a more liberal doctrine."[5]

Modern French support of the right of capture at sea is
practically confined to Hautefeuille and Ortolan. It is to be
observed, however, that the theory of the former depends
upon the now false premise that private property on land
is also subject to seizure.[6] The case of Ortolan is more peculiar, for while thoroughly Rousseaunian about the theory
of war,[7] and the exemption of private property on land, he
attempts to distinguish the latter from property at sea, in a
laborious and at times amusing way. He says, for example,

[1] Quoted by Hall from the *Moniteur* of Dec. 5th, 1806.
[2] "Il est à désirer," etc. *Mémoires de Napoléon*, t. 3, ch. 6, p. 304. The preamble of the Berlin decree is much more positive in its language. *Cf. infra*.
[3] Ed. 1862, II., 472.
[4] *Droit International*, § 1784. [5] *Ibid.*, § 1994.
[6] *Propriétés Privées des Sujets Belligérants sur Mer* (1860).
[7] *Cf. Règles Internationales et Diplomatie de la Mer* (1864). II., 27.

that at sea "no conquests or requisitions are possible. Yet the enemy must be injured in some manner" (*il faut bien nuire à l'ennemi d'une manière quelconque*).[1] This certainly cannot be an argument in favor of the capture of *private* property, for, as M. Ortolan himself admits, war is not a relation of individual to individual, and hence private merchants cannot be the enemies whom "*il faut nuire.*" He says, again, that seizing a ship and its cargo is a very different proceeding from seizing a man's household goods;[2] waiving which—it is not so very different after all—it must be remembered that it is not only the household goods, but factories, and stores, and things of a wholly professional kind, which are spared on land. Next, M. Ortolan refers to the fitness of the merchant marine of a state, both as to *matériel* and *personnel*, for immediate belligerent use.[3] But this argument, in these days of iron-clads, is obsolete as to the ship, and explains nothing about the confiscation of the cargo; while as for the crew, if they are to be made prisoners of war because they may at any moment join the navy, why not capture farmers on land on account of their intrinsic fitness for the army? Finally, M. Ortolan suggests that, were capture at sea abolished, a belligerent with a weak navy

---

[1] *Cf. Règles Internationales et Diplomatie de la Mer* (1864), II., 42. There is something humorous about M. Ortolan's theory that the absence of our real enemy justifies the beating of an innocent person who happens to be present. In the language of Bluntschli—"Allein niemais kann die Schwäche der rechtmässigen Kriegsmittel ein Grund sein, um die Zulässigkeit unrechtmässiger Kriegsmittel zu rechtfertigen." (*Das Mod. Völk.*, 45.) And Lavaleye says (*Rev. de Dr. Intern., infra.*) : "C'est comme si sur terre on brûlait syst'matiquement des fabriques, parce qu'elles sont une source de richesse pour l'ennemi."

[2] II., 43. In 1870 the wine in the cellars of Champagne was valued at 50,000.000 f., yet no one ever thought of it as subject to seizure by the Germans. Would M. Ortolan embrace the wine-casks within his description of household goods, or as he expresses it, "objets servant à l'usage d'un habitant paisible . . . où il a son foyer domestique?"

[3] *Dip. de la Mer.*, II., 49.

would simply withdraw its vessels of war from the seas;[1] but what possible harm that could do to any one but the weak belligerent itself, which would thus be unable to maintain blockades or to shut off contraband, is not made apparent. The means of prolonging the war, of course, are obtained, indirectly, from commerce; they are also obtained, however, from factories, yet the latter are exempt.

Though the French were the first to advocate what we shall now speak of as the modern theory of war, the writers of other continental nations did not hesitate to follow their lead.

At the outbreak of the Franco-German war, the King of Prussia issued to the German army a proclamation calling upon them to respect private property, and adding that he waged war against the French army, not the French people.[2] Heffter, writing shortly after the war, strongly discountenances the *confiscation* of private property at sea, although, indeed, he admits the right to seize and hold it in order that it may not benefit the enemy during the war.[3] His objection, however, to the French system in its entirety is only the rather pessimistic one that strong maritime powers could never be induced to give their consent.[4] On the other hand, Bluntschli adopts all the French theories as unques-

---

[1] *Dip. de la Mer.*, II., 49. See, for the same argument, Riquelme (*Elementos de Derecho Público Internacional*, Madrid, 1849, I., 136): "Fúndase esta diferencia en que en las guerras marítimas no hay otro medio de debilitar á un enemigo que encierra en sus puertos las escuadras y esquiva el combate, sino el de destruir su navegacion y su comercio."

[2] Proklamation vom 11 Aug., 1870: "Ich führe Krieg mit den französischen Soldaten, und nicht mit den französischen Bürgern."

[3] *Das Europäische Völkerrecht* (1873), § 139. Captor to have "kein Eigenthum . . . sondern lediglich das Recht der Beschlagnahme während der Dauer des Krieges."

[4] "Ein solches System würde allerdings mit gutem Grunde für eine fromme Chimäre zu erklären sein."

tionable. War is waged by states, not private persons,[1] and, as a logical and necessary consequence, capture of private property at sea is to be condemned.[2] Similarly Aegidi and Klauhold, in their *Frei Schiff unter Feindes Flagge* (Hamburg, 1866) condemn the old practice and look forward hopefully to the time when their state will be able " to obtain for the fundamental principle [of immunity for private property at sea] the consent of England and thus the recognition of the world."[3]

The Italian writers appear to be even more unanimous than the German. Azuni states the Rousseaunian theory of war without qualification,[4] and formulates certain maritime rules of which the first abolishes capture of private property other than contrabrand. Galiani calls it an "absurd and lamentable inconsequence" to allow capture at sea.[5] Ercole Vidari thinks that respect for private property is an absolute principle, applicable in war as well as in peace, on sea as well as on land. War is a relation of state to state, not of individual to individual.[6] Fiore[7] and Pierantoni[8] take the same view.

The sentiment of Holland, as expressed by Jan H. Ferguson, an eminent Dutch publicist and official, in 1884, is as follows: " War is a relation between States alone. * * * The state of war entails no *jus in personam* against every private individual in the state. * * * The savage maxim that when war is de-

[1] *Das Moderne Völkerrecht* (1878), §§ 530, 531; p. 35.
[2] *Id.*, § 665.
[3] *Einleitung*, 38.
[4] *Sistema Universale dei principii del diritto maritimo dell' Europa* (Ed. 1797, Triest), II., 303.
[5] *Dei doveri de principi neutrali* (1782).
[6] *Del rispetto della proprietà privata fra gli Stati in guerra* (1867), II., 2, 4.
[7] *Fiore* (Fr. ed.), II., 270; ch. VII, ch. VIII.
[8] *Rev. de Droit Intern.*, VII. (1875), 619. Rapport sur les Prises Maritimes.

clared between the two nations every individual member of the one is on the warpath against every person belonging to the other, is happily banished from the usages of warfare between civilized states."[1] Capture of private property at sea, therefore, is "anomalous" and a "conspicuous deviation from the principles of the law of war."[2]

Belgian writers, also, have voiced a ready assent to the modern theory. Laveleye, in a strong article in the *Revue de Droit International*,[3] the brilliancy of which called forth an astonishing tribute from the usually placid Calvo,[4] reviews all the arguments of Ortolan, and all the practice on the subject, and concludes that the old doctrine is already extinct on the continent and has not much longer to live anywhere. And Nys, in his *Guerre Maritime*,[5] speaking of the difference in the treatment of private property on land and at sea, exclaims, "The contradiction is flagrant, and * * * imperiously demands a reform."

In Russia the sentiment is the same. When President Monroe, in 1824, entered into negotiations with the French, British and Russian governments for the purpose of abolishing capture at sea, the Russian government, through Count Nesselrode, expressed hearty approbation of the scheme, but very naturally was unwilling to act alone.[6] Later, in 1856, when Mr. Marcy re-opened the question, the Russian chargé d'affaires at Washington, acting under the orders of Prince Gortschakoff,[7] replied that *the Emperor ac-*

[1] *Manual of Intern. Law for the Use of Navies and Consulates* (1884), II, 247, 248.
[2] *Id.*, II., 308. [3] VII. (1875), 560. [4] Calvo, § 1992.
[5] (Brussels, 1881), I., 134.
[6] Nesselrode to Middleton, Feb. 1, 1824.
[7] Gortschakoff to Stoeckl, Sept. —, 1856: "La proposition d'Amérique est dévelopée d'une manière si habile et si lumineuse qu'elle commande la conviction; . . . elle recevra un appui décidé de la part du représentant de Sa Majesté Impériale." Quoted in *Rev. de Dr. Int.*, VII., 569.

cepted, for his part, the condition on which the United States consented to abolish privateering—namely, that all private property on the seas should be respected.[1] Finally, in 1874, the Russian *projet* for a Declaration of Brussels embodied the following articles:

"1. An international war is a state of open hostility between two independent states and their armed and organized forces.

"2. The operations of the war must be directed only against the forces and means of war of the enemy state, and not against its subjects, as long as the latter take no active part in the war."

The various extracts which have been quoted may, it is believed, be taken as fairly representative of the spirit of continental publicists and diplomatists as it exists to-day. It remains before concluding this chapter to review briefly some of the practical attempts which men of action have made to abolish the capture of private property at sea.

The United States made the first effort. Principally through the endeavors of Franklin, who was strongly opposed to the old practice, the principle of the immunity of private property at sea was embodied in our treaty of 1785 with Prussia.[2] In 1792 the National Assembly of France resolved, that the executive power be "invited" to negotiate with foreign powers for the abolition of privateering and the free navigation of commerce. M. de Chambonas, consequently, issued a circular to the French diplomatic agents abroad, requesting them to discuss the matter with their respective governments. Only the United States made any satisfactory response; Jefferson, then Secretary of State, referring to and approving the treaty with Prussia, which was, perhaps, not unnatural on Jefferson's part, as he had helped to make it.

[1] Stoeckl to Marcy, Nov. 28th, 1856. (Aegidi, p. 20.)
[2] *Cf.* Art. 23.

In 1806 Napoleon recognized the fact that the right of capture of private property at sea was no longer properly a part of the law of nations, by apologizing for its exercise against England[1] and justifying it on the ground of reprisal. In 1823 the French refrained from capturing private property at sea in their war with Spain.[2] In the same year President Monroe renewed the efforts of the United States to make the new doctrine general. The favorable answer of Russia has been referred to; Chateaubriand for France replied similarly;[3] England alone escaped discussion of the question upon technical grounds which will be considered hereafter. In 1832, however, the latter power restored the ships captured in her war with Holland. In 1854 President Pierce announced his intention to continue the efforts of Monroe. In 1856 came the Declaration of Paris, abolishing privateering and confirming the rule that free ships make free goods. Immediately afterwards Marcy proposed his famous amendment to the Declaration, by abolishing all capture at sea except under the law of contraband and blockade; aud Russia's favorable reply to that proposal has been mentioned. In the same year (June 11) the Marcy amendment was incorporated into a treaty of commerce between Costa Rica and New Granada (Art. II.). In 1858 Sr. Da Silva Paranhos, Brazilian minister of foreign affairs, declared, that while the

[1] *Cf.* the preamble to the Berlin decree (Nov. 21, 1806):
"Napoléon, Empéreur des Français, roi d'Italie, considérant,
" 1. Que l'Angleterre n'admet point le droit des gens suivi universellement par tous les peuples policés;
" 2. Qu'elle répute ennemi tout individu appartenant à l'état ennemi et . . .
" 3. Qu'elle étend aux bâtiments et marchandises de commerce . . . le droit de conquête qui ne peut s'appliquer qu' à ce qui appartient à l'état ennemi— . . .
" Nous avons r'solu d'appliquer à l'Angleterre les usages qu'elle a consacrés," etc.

[2] "La marine royale," declared Chateaubriand, "ne prendra que les bâtiments de guerre espagnols; elle n'arrêtera les bâtiments marchands."

[3] Chateaubriand to Sheldon, Oct. 29, 1823. (Aegidi.)

world owed much to the Declaration of Paris, consistency required the adoption of the Marcy amendment *in toto*.[1] In 1859, by the treaty of Zurich, France restored the Austrian vessels captured during the war.[2] In 1860 England[3] and France[4] together proclaimed the principle in their war with China. In 1865 France restored vessels captured during the Mexican War. In the Seven Weeks' War of 1866 the immunity of private property at sea was declared by all three powers—Austria, Italy and Prussia;[5] Italy in fact having adopted a permanent rule of immunity, on condition of reciprocity.[6] Innumerable German diets, and chambers of commerce the world over, have resolved in favor of the new principle.[7] In 1870, at the outbreak of the Franco-Prussian war, the King of Prussia announced the exemption of French merchantmen; but on Jan. 12, 1871, Bismarck sanctioned a relapse into the old practice by way of reprisal. In 1871 the United States again embodied the immunity principle in a treaty, this time with Italy; the treaty is still (1897) in force.[8]

[1] *British and For. State Papers*, Vol. 48, p. 137.
[2] Art. 3. (Except such as had already been condemned.)
[3] Order in Council, March 7th, 1860.
[4] Dépêche du ministre des affaires étrangères du 28me Mars, 1860.
[5] " Les navires marchands et leur cargaisons ne pourront être capturés que s'ils portent de la contrebande de guerre ou s'ils essaient de violer un blocus effectif et déclaré."
[6] *Codice per la marine mercantile*, Art. 211 (1865).
[7] They are all collected in Aegidi, *Einleitung*, p. 24 n. The principal cities represented are London, Bremen, Lübeck, Rotterdam, Breslau, Bordeaux, Marseilles, Stuttgart, St. John's (N. B.), Liverpool, New York, Baltimore, Triest, Riga. The Bremen resolution is thus worded—
" * * * Beschliesst die Versammlung:
"(1) Die Unverletzlichkeit der Person und des Eigenthums in Kriegszeiten zur See, unter Ausdehnung auf die Angehörigen kriegführender Staaten, so weit die Zwecke des Kriegs sie nicht nothwendig beschränken, ist *eine unabweisliche Forderung des Rechtsbewusstseins unserer Zeit.* * * * "
[8] Art. 12. (Feb. 26, 1871.)

In 1877 the Institute of International Law, at Zurich, fully recognized the principle of immunity. And finally, in the code of the Institute for wars on land, recommended in 1880, the theory of individual enmity is distinctly negatived.[1]

In view of all these facts, it is respectfully submitted that Heffter cannot sustain his statement that the hope of abolition of capture at sea is a "pious chimera." Pious, yes. Chimera, no.

[1] Art. 1.

CHAPTER III

THE ENGLISH SCHOOL

THE continental writers, then, maintain that the theory of war has changed; that individuals who take no part in the war are no longer enemies; and that, consequently, the right of capture of private property at sea is no longer recognized in International Law.

English writers, on the contrary, are for the most part of the opinion that the theory of war has not changed; that individuals are still enemies; and that all the positive immunities which non-combatants enjoy owe their origin simply to humanity, and must be regarded as exceptions to a rule which, where not expressly suspended, still controls.

Perhaps the ablest, because the most serious, attack upon the continental theory is that of Mr. Hall. He maintains that the relation of enmity between individuals must still exist, because otherwise certain practices which are still recognized would be illegal. These practices are chiefly five—(1) the replacing of the civil government of an invaded state by military control, and the "making of any changes necessary" for the invader's "safety and success;" (2) the bombardment of fortified towns; (3) the right of contribution and requisition; (4) the right of compelling the personal service of members of the enemy state, and (5) the destruction of buildings and fields for military purposes.[1]

The first and fifth of these practices are, however, justified on the simple ground of military necessity. It is not because

[1] *Hall* (Ed. 1880), p. 59.

individuals are enemies—that is shown by the fact that no more damage may be done than is reasonably necessary for military operations. They are simply in the way, and so long as they remain in the way they must endure the temporary consequences. Such a relation is very far from a relation of enmity. It is as if I have a quarrel with X, and give notice to the world that I am going to shoot him, and thereupon A, B and C come and stand about X, and are accidentally hurt by the bullets.

The second practice is explained in substantially the same manner. Bombardment is a weapon aimed at individuals only incidentally. If the latter are enemies, why not bombard unfortified towns as well as fortified ones? Then the right of contribution and requisition has already been explained, and besides, there is, as has been seen, a strong tendency at the present time to pay for what is taken; and the supposed fourth practice, of compelling personal service, is, to say the least, of very doubtful legality. Certainly the citizens of either state cannot any longer be forced into the other's army or navy; and if they are occasionally compelled to hew wood and draw water, it does not follow that the compulsion is just and legal.

There are two reasons, concludes Mr. Hall, against the adoption of the continental theory. First, it is a fiction, for "to separate the state from the individuals which compose it, is to reduce it to an intangible abstraction."[1] A railroad company is an "intangible abstraction," but is that any reason for confusing it with its stockholders? It is the second reason of Mr. Hall, however, which is particularly worthy of note—the continental doctrine is *mischievous*, he says, because "*it is the argumentative starting-point of attack upon the right of capture of private property at sea.*"[2] And

[1] (Ed. 1880), p. 60.   [2] (Ed. 1880), p. 61.

this, it is conceived, is the trouble with the whole English school; and it is for this reason that a thoroughly unprejudiced opinion of the French theory of war is rarely obtained from an English publicist. The latter, in starting out to discuss the legitimacy of capture at sea, invariably begins by assuming it.

The late Sir Travers Twiss, therefore, is perhaps not entitled to as much weight on this subject as on most others. Besides, Twiss, like Hautefeuille, maintains the general confiscability of property on land,[1] and naturally, therefore, is not yet converted from the theory that "all the individual members of the one nation are enemies of the individual members of the other nation."[2] Similarly Phillimore, though calling war a "conflict of societies, that is, of corporate bodies recognizing and governed by law,"[3] evidently believes in individual enmity,[4] and declares the person of the "enemy," strictly speaking, liable to seizure and his property to confiscation. The other theory he considers to have a tendency toward the prolongation of the war.[5]

Phillimore, Twiss and Hall may be said to be fairly representative of the English school; but even in England there are dissenting voices. An early number of the Edinburgh Review[6] contains a striking appeal for the abolition of mari-

---

[1] *Law of Nations in Time of War*, p. 122.   [2] *Ibid.*, pp. 80, 82.

[3] *Commentaries*, III., 79.   [4] *Id.*, Preface, p. 37.

[5] Mr. Phillimore refers, with a frivolity which may be pardoned on account of its intrinsic humor, to the "famous but perhaps legendary precedent of the two Dutch admirals, who, commanding antagonistic fleets, sold powder to each other, and, commercially, contributed to their own destruction." (Preface, p. 39.) Phillimore differs from Bluntschli, who refuses to excuse a barbaric practice because it shortens the war (*Das Mod. Völk.*, p. 45). If it were the theory of nineteenth century statesmen to render wars barbarous in the hope of rendering them infrequent, it would have been false humanity to sign the Declaration of St. Petersburg or the Convention of Geneva.

[6] No. 15, p. 14.

time capture on the ground of humanity. Lord Palmerston in 1856, could "not help hoping" for such such abolition.[1] The letters of Mr. Cobden are full of passages showing his sympathy with the Marcy amendment to the Declaration of Paris. He regretted, as an Englishman, that the proposal did not originate in England,[2] and declared that if England did not at least support it, required as it was by the general sentiment of the age, "we should indeed deserve the title of the Chinese of the West."[3] It has been seen that the chambers of commerce all over England and the British possessions took the same view. Mr. Lindsay, M. P. from Lancaster, urged it constantly in the House of Commons. The report of the Select Committee on Merchant Shipping, ordered by the House of Commons to be printed Aug. 7, 1860, declared that "the time has arrived" for it. Altogether it is not necessary to be unduly optimistic to believe that the active opposition of England is on the wane. That opposition was formerly prompted by economic considerations, and since the adoption of the principle Free Ships Free Goods, the economic considerations seem rather to point the other way. Under the present law, in the wars of the future all the carrying trade of both belligerents would be driven into neutral bottoms, which, in case of war between England and another power, would always damage England more than her adversary in the ratio of the superiority of her carrying trade. If, moreover, we contrast the ease with which France or any continental nation could dispose of its produce through neutral ports in case of blockaded coasts, with the helpless position of England, if it should happen that her coasts were effectively blockaded, it will be seen that the change will

---

[1] Liverpool Address, Nov. 7th, 1856. (Aegidi.)
[2] Cobden to Bayley, Nov. 8th, 1856. (Aegidi.)
[3] Cobden to Carr, Dec. 15th, 1856. (Aegidi.)

benefit Great Britain more than any other power in the world.

To quote from a speech of Mr. Liddell's in the House of Commons:[1] "What did they do in the Russian war? They went to war with Russia in 1854. The first thing they did was to blockade the Baltic with a gigantic and expensive fleet, under pretence of distressing the enemy by cutting off the supplies which she furnished of raw material. They took a number of her ships, belonging chiefly to the poor inhabitants of the Baltic seaboard. * * * But did they stop Russian commerce? Why, the whole of the linseed, and the flax, and the tallow, and the hemp, the raw materials from Russia which England most wanted, were conveyed through neutral ports and arrived in this country at enhanced prices, which the consumer had to pay in consequence of the circuitous route which they had been obliged to travel."

In other words, blockade St. Petersburg, and Russia can use Königsberg; blockade Hamburg, and Germany will use Amsterdam; blockade Triest, and Austria will use Venice; but blockade the coasts of England and the produce must stay at home. That is why the policy of that country is likely soon to change.

In the meanwhile a small minority of foreign publicists adheres to the English school in its ancient notions of enmity. We have mentioned Hautefeuille and Riquelme.[2] Klüber[3] and Negrin[4] are referred to by Hall as taking the same view. And Bello, of the University of Chili, believed that the old

[1] March 11th, 1862 (Aegidi, p. 116.)

[2] "Son enemigos todos los súbditos de los Estados beligerantes"—(*Elem. de Der. Púb*, i., 135). But he adds: "Los enemigos se clasifican en enemigos inofensivos, forzados, y voluntarios." An "enemigo inofensivo," is something dangerously approaching a contradiction in terms.

[3] *Klüber*, § 232. His authorities are Grotius and Kant!

[4] *Tratado Elemental de Derecho Internacional Marítimo*, 141.

"maxims"[1] were still (in 1847) the better established, and that their "rigor" had been mitigated much in practice— nothing more. A good deal, however, has happened since 1847.

[1] "Segun el derecho de la guerra, * * * luego que un soberano la declara á otro, todos los súbditos del primero pasan á ser enemigos de todos los súbditos del segundo." *Principios de Derecho Internacional* (Caracas, 1847), 139.

CHAPTER IV

THE ATTITUDE OF THE UNITED STATES

THE Supreme Court of the United States has gone very far towards justifying the English assertion that this country agrees with England on the question of individual enmity. For example, it has held that property of the "enemy," found in the country at the breaking out of war, is "*stricti juris*" subject to confiscation.[1] And it has adopted for the United States the barbarous "commercial domicile" rule, which allows not merely subjects of the enemy state, but neutrals domiciled in the enemy's country, to be treated as enemies for the purposes of the law of capture at sea.[2] As

[1] Brown v. U. S., 8 Cranch, 110 (*semble*). Fortunately for the national honor, Chief Justice Marshall declared that an act of Congress would be necessary to render the confiscation complete, and reversed the circuit court's judgment of condemnation on the ground that no such act had been passed. The declaration of war gave the right to confiscate, but did not of itself operate as a confiscation. For comments on the unfortunate dictum mentioned in the text, see Woolsey, § 118, and Dana, note to Wheaton, § 355.

[2] The Prize Cases, 2 Black., 671; Miller v. U. S., 14 Wall., 268. This rule has never been shaken in England. "The following persons are enemies," says Lushington (*Manual of Naval Prize Law*, 1866, Art. 251): "(*a*) any person who has his domicile in the Enemy's territory, whatever be his Nationality by birth." And see the *Johanna Emilie*, Spinks, 12; the *Baltica*, Spinks, 266; the *Indian Chief*, 3 C. Rob., 18. What is thought of it elsewhere may be gathered from the criticism of Bluntschli (*Das Mod. Völk.*, § 532 n.): "Die ganze Theorie ist nur erdacht um möglichst viel Seebeute zu machen. Sie hat keinen Grund in den natürlichen Rechtsverhältnissen, und gelangt zuletzt zu der Abenteuerlichkeit, dass England das Eigenthum eines in den Vereinigten Staten wohnenden Engländers als feindliches Eigenthum behandelt, wenn England mit den Vereinigten Staten im Kriege ist." This monstrous doctrine has indeed been pushed so far as to lead to the condemnation of the property of *consuls* of one belligerent state

might be expected, certain of our writers have simply followed the Supreme Court and declared for individual enmity without, it may be, fairly hearing the other side. Thus Kent approves the old theory, and attempts to fortify it by the somewhat cumbrous fiction that "*every man is, in judgment of law, a party to the acts of his own government;*"[1] and Wheaton considers that a "perfect" war does not exist unless "all the members of both nations are authorized to commit hostilities against all the members of the other."[2] But the value of these opinions must depend largely upon that of the decisions upon which they are based; and it is to be remembered that during our war of 1812, when the first important decisions were rendered, the modern theory was not nearly so widely known or so strongly supported as it is now. The Supreme Court, being called upon not to legislate, but to declare the law as it found it, very naturally followed English traditions, and, with judicial conservatism, has held to them ever since, oblivious of the changes which fourscore years have brought. On the other hand, the executive department of our government has been hampered by no obligation, real or supposed, to adhere to English precedents, and it is therefore in the records of the Department of State, rather than in those of the Supreme Court, that the real sentiment of the country is to be found.

Now the history of American diplomacy, from beginning to end, is full of attempts to abolish the capture of private property at sea. Through the influence of Franklin, who always regarded it as a sort of piracy, and its strongest supporters, the English, as "the first piratical state in the

trading from the port in the other in which they are exercising their consular functions.

[1] *Abdy's Kent*, pp. 192, 193.

[2] *Elements*, § 296. See also Dana's note to § 355.

world,"[1] the following provision was incorporated into our treaty of 1785 with Prussia, in case of war:

"And all merchant and trading vessels employed in exchanging the products of different places and thereby rendering the necessaries, conveniences and comforts of human life more easy to be obtained, and and [sic] more general, shall be allowed to pass free and unmolested."[2]

When M. de Chambonas, in 1792, expressed the desire of the French government to secure the general adoption of such a principle, his efforts were warmly seconded by Jefferson, then Secretary of State. President Monroe, on December 2, 1823, sent the following message to the eighteenth Congress:[3]

"At the commencement of the recent war between France and Spain it was declared by the French government * * * that neither the commerce of Spain herself, nor of neutral nations, should be molested * * *. This declaration, which appears to have been faithfully carried into effect, concurring with principles proclaimed and cherished by the United States from the first establishment of their independence, suggested the hope that the time had arrived when the proposal for adopting it as a permanent and invariable rule in all future maritime wars might meet the favorable consideration of the great European powers. Instructions have accordingly been given to our ministers with France, Russia and Great Britain to make those proposals to their respective governments, * * * and an earnest hope is indulged that these overtures * * * will ultimately be successful."

The instructions referred to by the President had been

---

[1] Franklin's Works (Sparks), IX., 41, 467.

[2] Art. 23. Expired 1799. *Treaties and Conventions of the U. S.*, p. 905. The insertion of this article was authorized by Congress in its general plan for treaties adopted April 2, 1784. *Secret Journals of Congress, Foreign Affairs*, III., 456.

[3] *Am. State Papers, For. Rel.*, V., 245.

drawn up by John Quincy Adams, then Secretary of State, in the latter part of July. Mr. Adams declared that by an exception in the laws of war, "the reason of which it is not easy to perceive," private property at sea did not share the immunities of private property elsewhere; that the capture of such property was "a system of licensed robbery bearing all the most atrocious characters of piracy;" that its abolition had been one of the "favorite objects" of the United States "from the time when the United States took their place among the nations of the earth," and that the time had come to press these considerations "upon the moral sense" of other governments.[1]

Both the French and the Russian government expressed great willingness to make the matter the subject of a convention as soon as the consent of England could be obtained, but the course of the negotiations with the latter power was a most devious one. Our minister, Mr. Rush, seems at first to have entertained some hope of success,[2] but a more important maritime question, that of impressment, overshadowed this one, and resulted in an absolute disagreement of the plenipotentiaries. The British plenipotentiaries (Huskisson and Stratford Canning) refused to abandon formally the right of impressment, and gave it as their opinion, moreover, that "any discussion of the question at the present moment of general tranquillity would be altogether inadvisable."[3] Finally, at their twenty-second conference, Mr. Rush stated that the question of abolishing private war upon the ocean "was considered by him as standing apart from the other questions of maritime law * * * and he wished it understood that he was ready to treat on that question alone * * * ." The British plenipotentiaries said, in reply to this statement,

[1] Instructions to Mr. Rush, July 28th, 1823. (Aegidi.)
[2] Rush to J. Q. Adams, *Am. State Papers, For. Rel.*, V., 533 at 550.
[3] Protocol of 21st Conference, *Am. State Papers, For. Rel.*, V., 564.

"that under the circumstances, which prevented any present discussion of the questions of maritime law discussed in former negotiations, there would be manifest inconvenience in now going into a question of the same class."[1] The diplomatic relations between the two countries had now arrived at such an unpleasant stage that when, in 1826, Mr. Clay, Adams' successor as Secretary of State, wrote to Mr. Gallatin in London that the American government still desired, "with unabated force," all the things that Mr. Rush had proposed, he felt compelled to add a caution against pushing them as persistently as Mr. Rush had done.[2]

In J. Q. Adams' annual message, 1825, "abolition of private war upon the ocean" was again referred to as one of the cherished objects of the diplomacy of the United States.[3] President Pierce, in his message of December 4, 1854, declared that if other powers should concur in proposing immunity for private property at sea, "the United States will readily meet them on that broad ground." On July 28, 1856, after the United States had been asked to accede to the Declaration of Paris, Mr. Marcy wrote his famous note proposing the amendment of the Declaration by the abolition of all capture of private property at sea.[4] The withdrawal of this proposition by the Buchanan administration was due to no sympathy with the existing practice, for Buchanan himself had always opposed it, and Mr. Cass, in 1859, in his instructions to our minister at Paris, distinctly declared that it was "not adapted to the sentiments of the age in which we live."[5] At the beginning of our civil war, when it became manifest that the Confederate States were going to

[1] Protocol of the 22d Conference, *Am. State Papers, For. Rel.*, V., 564.
[2] Clay to Gallatin, June 19th, 1826. (Aegidi.)
[3] *Cf.* Von Holst's *Const. Hist. of the U. S.*, Appendix to *Int. Am. Conference*.
[4] Marcy to Count Sartiges, *Sen. Ex. Doc.* No. 5., 34th Cong., 3d Sess., p. 35.
[5] Mr. Cass to Mr. Mason, June 17th, 1859. (Aegidi.)

issue letters of mark, Mr. Seward did, it is true, offer to accede to the Declaration of Paris and abolish privateering without insisting on the Marcy amendment, hoping thus to bind the Confederate States; but he spoke of the bare Declaration as the "lesser good" and the Marcy amendment as the "greater,"[1] and when the negotiations were broken off, expressed a hope that they might, in some happier time, be resumed. Finally, in our treaty with Italy of 1871, we find the following provision (Art. 12):

"The high contracting parties agree that, in the unfortunate event of a war between them, the private property of their respective citizens and subjects, with the exception of coutraband of war, shall be exempt from capture or seizure, on the high seas or elsewhere."[2]

Mr. Hall, in his desire to show that the theory of individual enmity is adopted by our government, quotes article 21 of the United States' Instructions for the Government of Armies in the Field:

"The citizen or native of a hostile country is thus an enemy, as one of the constituents of the hostile state or nation, and as such is subject to the hardships of the war."

But Mr. Hall does not think it necessary to quote the next article:

"Art. 22. Nevertheless, as civilization has advanced, during the last centuries, so has likewise steadily advanced, especially in war on land, the distinction between the private individual belonging to a hostile country and the hostile country itself, with its men in arms. The principle has been more and more acknowledged that the unarmed citizen is to be spared in person, property and honor as much as the exigencies of war will permit." A strange enemy, whom we are enjoined to spare in "person, property and honor!" An

[1] Circular of April 24th, 1861.
[2] *Treaties and Conventions of the U. S.*, p. 584.

enemy, that is to say, with whom we have no quarrel; whose "enmity" exists neither in fact nor in law, but only by a figure of speech.

Mr. David Dudley Field, in his Draft of an International Code, says:

" War is a relation of nation to nation, or of community to community, and does not affect the relations of individuals * * * ." Of the contrary doctrine he says: " This legally imputed hostility is now so far mitigated by treaty provisions, and by ameliorations in the usages of war, and is so much opposed to the tendency of modern opinion, that it seems proper to recognize a different rule."[1] Similarly, among the numerous American publicists who do not follow Kent and Wheaton, is Dr. Woolsey, who calls the present practice " an antique usage " founded upon

> "the good old plan
> That they should get who have the power
> And they should keep who can,"

and who clearly and scientifically states the modern rule:[2]

"The true theory seems to be that the private persons on each side are not fully in hostile relations, but in a state of non-intercourse, * * * while the political bodies to which they belong are at war with one another, and they only."[3]

It cannot, then, be said that the "United States" is in favor of the English practice. Against our Supreme Court and its followers, Kent, Wheaton and Story, must be balanced such names as Adams, Jefferson, Franklin, Monroe, J. Quincy Adams, Pierce, Clay, Marcy, Cass, Seward, Lincoln —all declaring the contrary doctrine one of the principles "proclaimed and cherished by the United States from the first moment of their independence," not to mention such

---

[1] *Draft Outlines of an International Code* (N. Y., 1872), Art. 705, 705 n.
[2] *Am. Soc. Sc. Ass. Journal*, no. VII. (Sept. 1874).
[3] *Introduction to the Study of International Law*, § 119.

jurists as Field and Woolsey, who consider the English doctrine a thing of the past. If we have, in a certain sense, recognized that doctrine as still existing, we have spared no pains to show the world, and England in particular, that we do not agree with it. Which is the more remarkable, as it is matter of grave doubt whether abolition of capture at sea would at all accord with our belligerent interests.

SUMMARY

There are two conclusions from the foregoing chapters:

First, that the theory of individual enmity is no longer defensible; and, secondly, that the practice of capturing private property at sea is dying. It exists to-day, when it exists at all, for historical reasons purely; it is the logical result of a principle that is dethroned, and the student of history can deduce but one future for it. The end may be distant, it may be as Mr. Seward said in 1861, "even now near," but sooner or later the end is bound to come. Even now it is practically extinct upon the Continent. Germany, Italy, Austria, France, Russia—all have been prominent in promoting its downfall; it is the abhorrence of Belgium and of the Dutch. The United States has attacked it consistently from the first moment of its national existence. In a word, the overwhelming weight of the sentiment of the civilized world is against it; and when we have found the overwhelming weight of the sentiment of the civilized world, we have found the tendency of international law.

PART II

COMPARATIVE SKETCH OF PRIVATEERING BEFORE 1856

CHAPTER I

PRIVATEERING IN ENGLAND

* I

The Ante-Elizabethan Period

THE insular situation of England is responsible for her very ancient ambition to dominate the seas. The spirited foreign policy which she has always striven to maintain was checked by the loss of the French possessions in the 13th century, and the Anglo-Norman monarchs were compelled to abandon all hopes of acquiring a vast empire on the Continent; they turned, therefore, to the sea as the element which it would be at once the most easy and the most advantageous for them to rule. Britain, thrice conquered from without, could not itself be safe from foreign invasion without such dominion; and it could exercise no influence on continental politics without commanding the only avenue of approach to the Continent. Moreover, the sea-faring tastes of a large portion of the population, hardened and dedicated to the sea through generations of struggling with the Danes, gave promise that marine dominion would not be hard to acquire; and shaped for the English sovereigns the policy in which they have persevered with such success till the present day. It is on this subject—the mastery of the seas—that the national vanity has ever shown itself most monstrous. Said Lord Coke, "The King's navy exceeds all others in the world for three things, viz., beauty, strength and safety. * * * Amongst the ships of other nations, they are like lions amongst silly beasts, or falcons amongst fearful fowle."[1] The dramatic incident of the English admiral who fired upon the vessel in which Philip II. was coming to marry Mary, because, forsooth, it had not lowered its flag in "English" waters, was simply another exhibition of the same sentiment, which, indeed, is so indestructible that even after its rude shock in 1812, Englishmen were to be found triumphantly accounting for the maritime successes of the Americans on the ground of the "English blood in their veins."

The original pretensions of England amounted not merely to control, but to government, of the sea. During the reign of John a mandate was issued to the fleet to seize and make prize of all foreign ships found on English seas. And all foreign vessels, *wherever they were met*, were to be required to strike their colors by way of salute to the English flag. Only long afterwards, when Spain and Portugal had surpassed England in the extravagance of their claims, did the latter power reverse her early policy and contend for *mare liberum*. Since that change of principles, which occurred in the reign of Elizabeth, her effort has been simply to maintain so great a naval superiority as to be able to dictate to the world on questions of maritime law.

The royal navy, as a permanent institution, is not older than the fourteenth century.[2] Previous to that time, the practice of the Norman kings had been to depend on the coast towns, and particularly on Hastings, Romney, Hythe,

[1] Fourth Institute.

[2] Southey (*Lives of the Admirals*, II.) places the time when the king's ships "became a distinct class" as late as 1497. But, in 1328, Edward III. had 500 vessels (Nicolas, *History of the Royal Navy*, I.), and apparently the navy never quite died out from his time till that of Elizabeth. Of course, there were spasmodic attempts at a navy very much earlier. Alfred was in possession of quite a large one; so was Henry I. in 1106; and in 1190 the fleet which bore Cœur-de-Lion to the Holy Land contained, besides 38 galleys and 150 small vessels furnished for war, nine ships of "extraordinary size."

Dover and Sandwich, known as the Cinque Ports, to furnish a sufficient number of ships to tide them over any emergency.[1] In 1242, the King simply ordered the vessels of the Cinque Ports to commit every possible injury upon the French at sea, thus practically converting every vessel in those ports into an uncommissioned privateer. The consequences are interesting to note: "Not satisfied with obeying these commands, the sailors of the Cinque Ports * * * slew and plundered like pirates, as well their own countrymen, as foreigners."[2] In the succeeding year, 1243, the first privateers' commissions of which there is any evidence in the public records[3] were granted, in the form of "licenses," by Henry III.; the one to Geoffney Piper and the other to Adam Robernolt and William le Sauvage.

The latter was worded as follows:

"Relative to annoying the king's enemies. The King to all, etc., greeting. Know ye that we have granted and given license to Adam Robernolt and William le Sauvage, and their companions whom they take with them, to annoy our enemies by sea or by land, wheresoever they are able, *so that they share with us the half of all their gain;* and therefore we command you neither to do nor suffer to be done, any let, damage or injury to them or their barge, or other ship or galley that they may have; and they are to render to the King, in his wardrobe, the half of all their gains."[4]

In this document there is, it will be perceived, no use of the terms "mark," "countermark," or "reprisal." Robernolt and Le Sauvage had suffered no private wrongs at the hands of the subjects of France, for which they sought compensation. Their prospective prizes are spoken of as "gain."

[1] Thus, Hastings was required to furnish 21 ships, of 20 men or above; and each of the other four towns 5 ships, with 21 men or above. Hervey, *Hist. of the Royal Navy*, I., 61.

[2] Sir H. Nicolas, *Hist. of the Royal Navy*, I., 200.

[3] *Id.*, I., 239.

[4] Rot. Patent. 27 Hen. 3, m. 16. Quoted by Nicolas, I., 239, with the remark: "*Privateers, the disgrace of civilized states,* are thus shown to have existed in the thirteenth century."

They are, therefore, privateers,[1] pure and simple. It was half a century later before the first letter of mark, or what is supposed to be the first,[2] was issued in England. In 1295, one Bernard D'Ongressil, of Bayonne, then part of the English dominions, had a vessel, the St. Mary, laden with figs, etc., driven by stress of weather into Lagos, Portugal. Some Portuguese sailors from Lisbon seized the vessel and cargo, and after committing various depredations, declared them "confiscated." Vessel and cargo were sold, and when the matter came to the ears of the King of Portugal, the latter, instead of punishing the robbers, appropriated to himself one-tenth of the spoil. D'Ongressil, who had suffered damage to the amount of about £700, and who was unable to obtain any redress in Portugal, "prayed Sir John of Brittany, then lieutenant of Gascony, to grant him letters of marque; literally, 'license of marking the men and subjects of the kingdom of Portugal, and especially those of Lisbon, and their goods by land and sea,' until he had obtained compensation (*licentia marcandi homines et subditos de regno Portugalliæ*, etc.)."[3] In June, 1295, the king's lieutenant accordingly granted D'Ongressil, his heirs, successors and descendants, authority for five years "to mark, retain and appropriate" (*possit marchare, retinere et sibi appropriare*) the people of Portugal and their goods, until he had obtained satisfaction. On the third of the following October the king confirmed the authority, with the provision that if there should be any surplus, *i. e.*, if D'Ongressil should take more than his claim, it should be accounted for to the king.

The peculiar use of the word "marcare" or "marchare"

[1] The term "privateer" was not known at this time, nor indeed for nearly four centuries afterwards. Probably the first use of the word is that occurring in a letter of Sir Leoline Jenkins of Dec. 5th, 1665 (*Life of Sir L. J.*, II., p. 727). See Twiss, *War*, 375.

[2] See Campbell, *Lives of the Admirals*, I., 105, and Nicolas, I., 276.

[3] Nicolas, *Hist. of R. N.*, I., 276.

in this connection, has led some writers to the conclusion that here is the etymological source of the term "letter of mark." In other words, a letter of mark is a license to *mark*, to set apart, the goods of the tortfeasor nation and its subjects from those of all the other nations in the world, as a source of compensation for the tort. But the more probable origin of the term is to be found in the German mark (althochdeutsche *marcha*), "boundary" or "frontier." When a subject had been wronged by a fellow-subject, and the prince was too weak or too inert to punish the wrong-doer, he frequently delivered to the plaintiff what were called letters of reprisal, which substantially allowed him to take the law into his own hands and keep what he could get. If the wrong-doer, instead of a fellow-subject, happened to be a foreigner, the letters were known as letters of mark and reprisal, or shortly, letters of mark, from the fact that they contained permission to cross the frontier (mark) and seize the goods of the wrong-doer abroad.[1] If the derivation is from anything else, it is difficult to understand why the term letter of mark was never used in connection with anything but international seizures. If mark has no reference to frontier, why not call permission to prey on the goods of a fellow-subject a letter of mark? For it is just as true as in the case of an alien that his goods are being "marked and set apart" for seizure.

About these early letters of mark there are several interesting things to be noted. In the first place, they were absolutely and essentially distinct, at the beginning, from the "license" or "commission" of a privateer, applying that term to the kind of vessel used by Robernolt and Le Sauvage

[1] Littré, *Dict. de la Langue Française;* Webster's *Dict.*; Woolsey, *Internat. Law*, § 121. Still other, and not a few, authorities are content with the shallow explanation that the term was primarily French; *i. e.*, that lettre de marque = stamped letter, in precise analogy to lettre de cachet, or letter sealed. See *Johnson's Encycl.*, *The Century Dict.*, etc.

in 1243. The privateer was used only in time of war; the letter of mark was of no value[1] to any one except in time of peace, which in theory it did not break.[2] The avowed object of the privateer was "gain," half of which, be it great or small, must be paid to the king; there was no limit to the amount of booty which it might acquire. The object of the letter of mark was compensation, more than which it had no right to take, and the surplus beyond which, if any, had to be accounted for; as for the king, he received nothing at all. Privateers were to "annoy the king's enemies." The letter-of mark was to redress a purely private wrong. The king, in granting the privateer's license, exercised a belligerent right; in issuing the letter of mark he conferred a sort of property grant, which ran to the "heirs, successors and descendants" of the grantee. Two things more dissimilar in theory it would be hard to find; yet in a few years from this time we find them in a state of hopeless confusion; and to-day the commission of a privateer is spoken of indiscriminately as a commission, a license, a letter of mark (marque, mart) or script of mart. Add to this that the term is some-

[1] In June, 1778, *lettres de représailles* were given by the French king to Sieurs Basmarin and Raimbaux, who had had eleven vessels taken by the English before any declaration of war, on the pretence that they were carrying aid to the American colonies. The alliance between the latter and Louis XVI. being soon after made known, Basmarin and Raimbaux complained that they could not use their letters of reprisal on account of the war. Lebeau, *Nouveau Code des Prises*, I., 104 n.; II., 45.

[2] A letter-of-mark was one of those peculiar things spoken of in the old books as "Measures Short of War." Now, the conception of war without a declaration having been at last developed, thanks to the English practice in the 18th century, we no longer call such things as the issuance of a letter-of-mark in time of peace a "measure short of war"; we call it an *act* of war itself. Formerly, however, the action was regarded as leaving the peace unbroken, because war could not exist unless formally declared. "La délivrance de lettres de représailles ne rompait nullement la paix entre les deux états."—Nys, *La Guerre Maritime* (Brussels, 1881), p. 147. *Cf.* also Carlos Testa, *Dr. Pub. Int. Mar.* (1866), p. 160.

times printed in full, "letter of mark and reprisal," and sometimes called "letter of reprisal" or "letter of mark" for short; and that it has come to cover (1) the piece of paper, (2) the ship, and (3) another totally different kind of ship, viz., a peaceful merchant vessel armed to resist attack;[1] and it will be seen how hopeless must be all endeavor to set the terminology right. Just how the confusion arose it is hard to say. In 1295, as has been shown, a privateer and a letter of mark were clearly distinct, at least in England. Probably the course of affairs was something like this: Whenever a war broke out, each party always claimed to be the party aggrieved, and when it justified its acts of hostility at all, it did so by connecting them in some way with the notion of "reprisals."[2] Of course, from reprisals to mark was but a step; and as the practice of a letter of mark was almost identical with that of a privateer, the two ideas became fused.

The issue of letters of mark, in the original sense, was very frequent during the early part of the fourteenth century. There being no regular navies of any size, the seas were infested with pirates and quasi-piratical adventurers of all nations, who despoiled with more or less discrimination those who came in their way. "A mariner called Dennis was committed to Newgate in 1227, for being present when a Spanish ship was plundered and her crew slain at Sandwich."[3] Some time later nine marks were given to "Alexander the goldsmith and seven companions, and a woman called Margaret,"[4] *for their support*, they having been "despoiled" by rovers from the Cinque Ports.

[1] See, for this use of the term, Bouvier's *Law Dict.; Am. & Eng. Enc. of Law;* Coggeshall's *Hist. of Am. Privateers*, etc.

[2] In England the practice is to issue an Order in Council directing "general reprisals" against the hostile power; this was done as recently as 1854, at the opening of the Russian war. See, on this practice, Twiss, *War*, p. 334, and De Burgh, *Maritime Int. Law* (London, 1868).

[3] Nicolas, *Hist. R. N.*, I., 233. [4] *Ibid.*

The conduct of the Cinque Ports, in using the king's permission to cruise against his enemies as an opportunity for piracy, has already been noticed. From 1303 to 1338 the English pirates were unusually active and daring.[1] In the latter year one "Gomyz," a Spanish envoy, was "spoiled" on his way to England, and actually confined in a dwelling on shore: on the matter becoming known to the king, he directed the spoilers to be arrested as for "contempt."[2] The kings of France and Spain, and the counts of Flanders, were in a constant state of altercation with England on the subject of the wrongs done to their commerce by the English pirates. In 1340 Edward III. had to pay "out of his own pocket" for spoils committed by his British subjects on his Genoese allies.[3] On the other hand, in 1318 the French Admiral of "Caleys" committed spoil on the English; and the Spaniards and Portugese retaliated constantly. The result was a great stream of applications, on the part of the innocent English, for letters of mark; and after they had satisfied their claims from innocent Spaniards, French, Flemish or Portuguese, the latter turned naturally to their governments for letters of counter-mark, which were almost invariably granted. Yet, as has been seen, no one ever thought of this state of things as war.

At this time letters of mark were issued by the chancellor, and it was one of the most important and honorable functions of that officer[4] to grant them. But with the introduction of the title of admiral in 1300[5] there gradually sprang up in

[1] In 1315 some Flemings were spoiled at Oswald House; in 1321 Brittany uttered threatening complaints; Aragon followed suit in 1324, Castile in 1333; France in 1335; and Genoa 1336.

[2] *Select Pleas in the Court of Admiralty* (Publications of the Selden Society, vol. 6 for 1892), Introduction.

[3] *Ibid.*   [4] *Ibid.*

[5] The Black Book of the Admiralty is wrong in the supposition that the title of admiral antedates the fourteenth century in England. See *Select Pleas*, etc. In

connection with his office a sort of marine jurisdiction which not very long after developed into the court of admiralty. In 1295 the master of a ship was summoned before De Sestas, admiral of the "Baion" fleet, and subjected to a fine. On the other hand, in England proper, the common law courts, the king's council and the chancellor, all jealous of the new jurisdiction which encroached upon their own, did what they could to hinder its development. In 1314 French piracy claimants were told to sue at common law; in 1320 Flemish piracy claims were arbitrated.[1] But in 1340 occurred the battle of Sluys, which left the English, for the time, masters of the northern seas; and the consequent increase of their maritime pretensions[2] led to a sudden dignifying of the post of admiral, and an extension of its administrative and judicial power. The first reference to proceedings in a case of spoil before the admiral, would seem to indicate the year 1357 as the time when the court of admiralty as such began.[3] From this time it gradually took cognizance of nearly all marine matters, and, of course, it robbed the chancellor of his right to issue letters of mark.

The piratical conduct of the Cinque Ports continued all through the fourteenth and the early part of the fifteenth century. Their adventurers, on account of their incalculable

1295 (23 Ed. I.) one De Sestas is made admiral (*admirallus*) of the "Baion" fleet. But later, in 1297, the titles "Keeper of the Sea Coasts" and "Captain of the King's Mariners" are used instead. And the first admiral who existed in England proper was Gervase Alard, admiral of the fleet of the Cinque Ports, 1300. (*Wardrobe Accounts*, 29 Ed. I., *Select Pleas*, etc.)

[1] *Select Pleas*, etc.

[2] There is no mistake about the claim of sea sovereignty (*Superioritas, Custodia, Admirallitas*) put forward by the English after the battle of Sluys. In 1372 a petition to parliament actually contained the monstrous statement that "then and in all times past all countries held and called the King of England 'King of the Sea'—(*touz les pays tenoient et appelloient nostre avan dit seignour le Roi de la mier*)." *Select Pleas*, etc.

[3] *Ibid.*

utility in time of war, were not restrained by the king in time of peace, for fear, perhaps, that they might fall out of practice. Their continued depredations, however, became too troublesome to the English themselves to be allowed to continue; and with the advent of Henry V. in 1413, a statute was passed making piracy high treason.[1] But the hold which the custom had gained upon the seaports, made it difficult to check; and the men of good birth who supported it with their brains or capital and derived large incomes from it in return, kept the institution from going to utter ruin. In 1425, Marcellus, abbot of St. Augustine in Canterbury, was *fined* for piracy.[2]

In the fifteenth and the early part of the sixteenth century, privateering and piracy are closely allied. The conduct of privateers and pirates was about the same; the only difference being that the former had a commission, or letter of mark, as it was now beginning to be called, while the latter had not. Now this letter of mark was an expensive luxury. From 1360, when Sir John Beauchamp was appointed admiral of all the fleets,[3] there had developed, in addition to the more ancient office of Lord Warden of the Cinque Ports, the dignity of Lord High Admiral. As in France, this honor was usually bestowed upon some one absolutely ignorant of nautical matters, nearly always some member of the royal family. In 1525 it was held by young Prince Henry, a child of six. This nominal head of the admiralty derived a large income from his position; and, *inter alia*, always shared largely in the prizes taken by private adventurers who acted under a commission. The Lord Warden of the Cinque Ports also had a share; so that it was much more profitable to cruise against the enemy without a commission than with one. Neither was the danger incurred

[1] *Stat.* 2 Hen. V. c. 6.   [2] Southey, *Lives of the Admirals*, vol. II.
[3] *Select Pleas*, etc.

very much greater; for while a captured pirate was, as a matter of course, disposed of at the yard-arm, a captured privateer was very likely to be so treated as well, the duty of giving quarter not being as yet generally recognized. As the restrictions against pirates, however, came to be more and more zealously enforced, and as more and more of the booty taken by privateers came to be appropriated by the Lord Warden and the Lord High Admiral, the falling off of the English marine became but too noticeable; and led, in 1544, to heroic measures on the part of Henry VIII. The latter being then at war with France, issued a general call for privateers; requiring them to obtain no license and to give no security, but simply to arm, equip, and fall upon the French wherever found; *and they were to have the whole property in the prizes which they took, without any bonus for the Lord High Admiral or the Lord Warden of the Cinque Ports.* Henry VIII. in 1544 foreshadowed the Prize Act of Anne; and the consequences of his system foreshadowed the consequences of hers. First, a general awakening, then an enormous activity of the private adventurers, nearly every able-bodied man in England who owned a boat equipping it for war;[1] momentary annihilation of hostile commerce; and then the abuses with regard to neutrals. The English privateers covered the seas; French merchantmen became few and far between; and rather than go home bootyless, the adventurers fell upon the Spanish, the Portuguese and the Flemings. However, they had answered their purpose, and were recalled.

[1] " Adventurers," says Southey (*Lives of the Admirals*, II., 214), " hastened to take advantage of the general license; and being so numerous, they scoured the Channel with extraordinary good fortune. More than 300 French prizes were brought into English ports: and so large a part of their cargoes was brought to London that the Grey Friars' Church was filled with wine, and both St. Austin's aud the Black Friars' with herrings and other fish intercepted on the way to France."

One more curious fact deserves to be chronicled before we pass to the Elizabethan period. It appertains to the reign of Mary, and tends to show the hardiness of the early privateers and their equality for most purposes with ships of war. In 1557, during the struggle with France and Scotland, "the trade of the kingdom suffered considerably from the swarm of privateers which issued from the different ports of Scotland."[1] Sir John Clare, Vice-Admiral of England, was sent "to those parts with twelve sail of ships, to revenge these insults;" but the bold Scotch adventurers met and defeated him, and during the action "the boat which he was on board over-set, and himself, with several others, were drowned."[2]

2

From the Reign of Elizabeth to the Prize Act of Anne (1708).

"In spite of its insular position and its pretensions," says a French historian,[3] "England never played a great part on the seas before the end of the sixteenth century." The battle of Sluys had established her maritime supremacy over France, which, dismembered and disorganized, was in no condition to regain it, but the Spanish and Portuguese remained masters of all the seas except those in the immediate neighborhood of England, and were everywhere recognized as the first naval powers of the day.

Theretofore the interests of Spain and England had not clashed. But with the accession of Elizabeth, and the restoration of Protestantism, the hatred of Spain which had begun to develop in England during the reign of Mary burst

---

[1] Hervey, *History of the R. N.*, I., 325.   [2] *Ibid.*

[3] " Malgré sa position insulaire, son commerce avec les Flandres, et ses prétentions, qui datent de loin, à la souveraineté des mers, l'Angleterre n'avait pas joué un grand rôle maritime avant la fin du seizième siècle." Duneaud, *Hist. de la Marine Française*, ch. i.

forth with violence. The religious differences arising from the inquisition on the one side and the persecution of the Catholics on the other, contributed, as well as Elizabeth's refusal to wed with Philip II., to embitter the political controversy arising out of the Spanish claim to exclude foreigners, and particularly English, from the New World, under the papal bull of 1493. So that, while war was not declared until 1588, there was a condition of private hostility much earlier. The rich Spanish possessions in America offered a tempting bribe to the privateering instincts of the men of the coast towns; and the sea dogs, as they were called, with the secret connivance of Elizabeth's government, committed enormous depredations upon Spanish commerce.

The practice of Sir Francis Drake may, perhaps, be considered as typical. In 1568, Drake was ruined in an expedition of Sir John Hawkins which committed an unprovoked attack on San Juan de Ulloa and was defeated. A naval "divine" having told Drake that he would be justified in making good his losses at the expense of the king of Spain, he commenced by two or three voyages to the West Indies, where he obtained "some store of money by playing the seaman and the pirate."[1] Then followed his expedition of 1577 to the South Sea. During this memorable voyage, he entered the port of Valparaiso, and after taking a Spanish ship, plundered the port.[2] At Tarapacá the English found

[1] A more excusable case was that of Andrew Barker, whose property was seized, in 1576, by the Inquisition in the Canaries, and who "fitted out two barks to revenge himself." The state papers of Elizabeth's reign are full of *querelae*, or *ex parte* proceedings for letters of reprisal against Spain and Portugal. *Select Pleas*, etc.

[2] The circumstances of the taking of this ship are interesting. It appears that the Spaniards, on the entry of the English, in the simplicity of their souls took them for friends, "saluted them with beat of drum and made ready a jar of Chili wine to drink with them;" but the English coming on board, one of them cried to the nearest Spaniard, "Down, dog" (*abaxo perro*), and all began to lay about them. Southey, *L. of the Adm.*, III., 143.

a Spaniard lying asleep, with thirteen bars of silver beside him, and Southey significantly says, "*no personal injury was offered to the man.*" At Arica, Drake took two ships with their cargoes; and on his return home Elizabeth, to whom all of these things were known, visited his ship and knighted him.[1]

In 1585, Drake's tastes being no longer satisfied with mere robbery, he took to arson. Santiago and St. Augustine were burned, and St. Domingo and Carthagena were compelled to pay a heavy ransom to escape the like fate. Nombre de Dios, Rio de la Hacha and Santa Marta were all burned by Drake at various times. His last expedition, that of 1596, was the most unsuccessful of all, the Spaniards repulsing him in several places; and in the course of it, he died. His death is said by the Spaniards to have been the result of mortification at his ill success.[2]

The exploits of Cavendish are of a more barbarous character even than those of Drake. In 1586, on an expedition to the South Sea, he finds a little Spanish colony starving; he sails away and leaves it in its misery. After plundering two settlements, he at last falls in with some Spanish vessels, of which he makes prize; some of the prisoners are tortured;[3] those who are not killed are put on shore. Paita

[1] The absolute approval which Elizabeth accorded to Drake's piracies is evidenced by her remark as she presented the sword: "We do account that he which striketh at thee, Drake, striketh at us."

[2] The Spanish admiral, Don Bernaldino Delgadillo de Avellaneda, wrote to Pedro Florez in 1596, "que Francisco Draque murio en Nombre de Dios, de pena, de aver perdido tantos Baxeles y gente." This letter was characterized by Mr. Henrie Savile, Esq. (*Hakluyt's Voyages*, IV., 75), as a "Libell of Spanish lies;" and so indeed it would seem, for the Don also states, incautiously enough, that Drake's fleet fled before him *leaving their oars behind;* whereas it is conclusively proved that there was not a galley in the expedition.

[3] " But he was fain to cause them to be tormented with their thumbs in a wrinch . . . also he made the old Fleming believe that he would hang him, . . . and yet he would not confess" (*Hakluyt*, IV., 316 at 324). One of the prisoners actually did have a rope put about his neck, whereby he was "pulled up a little from the hatches."

and Guatulco, little settlements aggregating 300 houses, are both burned; at Puna island he sinks a ship "with all her furniture."

Another famous adventurer was George Clifford, third Earl of Cumberland. His first expedition was sent out under one Withrington, for the purpose of plundering Bahia; but the gallant defence of the Jesuits with their Indian archers compelled it to return unsuccessful, the resolution to do which "was taken heavily by all the company, for very grief to see my lord's hopes thus deceived and his great expenses cast away."[1] This failure, however, was more than balanced by the success of Cumberland's voyage of 1589, in which he took no less than thirteen prizes,[2] including one laden with sugar and silver, and having on board a private venture of the captain's to the amount of 25,000 ducats. The town of Fayal, about 500 well-built houses, was abandoned at his approach, and ransomed for 2000 ducats, "mostly in church plate." So great was the terror inspired by his approach, that while he was yet miles away the governor of Graciosa, to "deprecate a visit," sent him sixty butts of wine. In 1592, on his fourth voyage, he obtained, by threats of torture, some information from a captured vessel which led to the taking of the *Madre de Dios*, a very large and rich East Indiaman, to which, however, the greatest courtesy was extended. He "sent them his own chirurgeons," and freely dismissed the captain and most of his followers, who, however, "had the ill hap to fall in with other English cruisers who took from them, thus negligently dismissed, 900 diamonds, besides other odds and ends."[3] Those were profitable days for the

[1] Southey, *L. of the Adm.*, III., 3.

[2] Two of these prizes were French, but, "belonging to the party of the League, were deemed fair prize" (Southey, III., 4). Similarly, on his fifth voyage, in 1593, he captured two French vessels from St. Malo, for "that port held for the League; the ships, therefore, were accounted Spaniards." (*Id.*, p. 24.)

[3] Southey, III., 21.

English privateers. Yet, out of 159,000 l. which the *Madre de Dios* was worth, only 36,000 l. went to the earl and his crew. The queen, one of whose ships was in the engagement, took the rest.

On his last voyage, in 1597, Cumberland took the town and fort of Porto Rico. "As he designed to make this city and harbor his station, from whence to cruise upon the Spanish coast, he drove out all the inhabitants."[1] And yet Monson tells us, with an air of great pride, and as a proof of the good discipline and courtesy required by the earl from his followers, that he "*publicly disgraced* a good soldier for *over-violent spoiling a gentlewoman of her jewels.*"[2]

The defeat of the Armada established the maritime supremacy of England over Spain, as that over France was already assured; and for some years afterwards the English privateers ruled the sea with an iron hand. The queen having resolved to attack Spain, organized for that purpose a large expedition consisting almost entirely of privateers, "the queen only furnishing a few ships, and giving the enterprise the sanction of her authority."[3] Incidentally, this also furnished the queen with an excuse for taking the lion's share of the booty. The ostensible purpose of the expedition was to recover Portugal for Donna Antonia; in which design it was foiled by a large Spanish fleet which had assembled at Lisbon. Here the privateering character of the expedition made itself apparent. "The object of the expedition being private again," says Hervey,[4] "*a scrupulous adherence to the rights of neutral powers was not likely to be observed;* here, therefore, *by way of idemnification*, they seized upon sixty hulks, or fly boats, belonging to the German Hanse-Towns." The interesting part of the matter is the fact that the English government supported and attempted

---

[1] Hervey, *Hist. R. N.*, I., 469.   [2] Monson (*Tracts in Churchill*), 193.
[3] Hervey, *Hist. R. N.*, I., 454, 455.   [4] *Ibid.*

to justify this act, so that "at length a total breach between England and the Hanse-Towns ensued."[1]

In addition to the outrageous conduct of this Spanish expedition, Drake and Cumberland were very active, and spread terror among the Spanish colonies. The naval successes were not all on the side of the English; for Sir Richard Grenville was captured by the Spaniards, with his ship, the *Revenge*, in 1591; and five years later Sir Richard Hawkins met the same fate. But about this time Raleigh landed in Trinidad and burnt San José de Oruño, putting all the garrison to the sword;[2] and in the same year (1593), Sir Amyas Preston ravaged and burnt Porto Santo and put Cumaná to ransom. Raleigh, coming upon the unfortunate town soon afterwards, would not ransom it again, but burnt it to the ground. Caracas was set on fire by Preston, but not completely destroyed.[3]

Altogether, at the death of Elizabeth in 1603, it might fairly be said that England had attained her ambition and was mistress of the seas. The royal navy had been almost doubled; but that had played a very unimportant part in the naval history of the reign, nearly all the triumphs of which had been due to private adventurers. The commercial marine had increased enormously. The New World had been opened up to English trade and civilization, and the strength of Spain was broken forever. Everywhere on the seas an English cruiser was known and feared.

[1] Hervey, *Hist. R. N.*, I., 454, 455.   [2] *Hakluyt*, IV., 120.

[3] Southey, *Lives of the Admirals*, IV., 294. In spite of these excesses, Gibson mournfully complains of the "gentlemen captains" of Elizabeth's time, in the following language: "I find punctillues of honor oft insisted on by gentlemen, and the loss of many a good design; when, on the other hand, the tarrpawlings observe noe grandure, but, like devells, count themselves most happy that can doe most and soonest mischief to their enemys." Southey, V., 207. What a worthy privateer this Gibson would have made, to whom the exploits of Raleigh appeared full of "punctillues of honor"!

With the accession of the Stuarts in 1603 there came a change. A treaty of peace and alliance was concluded with Spain; and as James I. and his Most Catholic Majesty were really friendly, without any *arrière pensée*, the English freebooters felt that they were doomed. A few of the more daring spirits continued their depredations for a while, but the example of Raleigh showed that the king was honestly trying to preserve the peace, and finally checked their ardor. The unfortunate Raleigh, taking it for granted that James, like Elizabeth, would secretly connive at violations of the treaty with Spain, ventured to attack the Spanish settlement of San Tomas, on the Orinoco. The governor of Guiana, Diego Palameque de Acuña, having heard of the approaching visit of one "Walter Reali," had prepared himself for defence; but the English were the first to break the peace, and after a short conflict, in which the governor was killed, they burnt the town and the surrounding plantations, even the churches and the convent not being spared. As they embarked for their return, carrying with them all the public papers, the church ornaments, and 2000 reales in gold, they exultantly told the Indians that they would return the following year and complete the destruction of the Spaniards. News of this exploit having reached London, the Spanish ambassador became so violent in his complaints that James I. was obliged to throw Raleigh into prison, where, as is well known, he was ultimately executed. The shock to the national spirit occasioned by the execution of Raleigh was very great,[1] and privateering as an institution began from that moment to decline.

During the seventeenth century the principal rivals of the English for marine supremacy were the Dutch,[2] from whom

[1] See *Hume's Hist. of Eng.*, vol. VI., p. 99; and Hervey, *Hist. R. N.*, vol. II., p. 37.

[2] The rivalry which existed between the English and the Dutch is well illus-

no such rich booty was to be gained as that which Drake and Raleigh had brought from the Spanish possessions in America. The share of the Lord High Admiral,[1] therefore, began to be more and more oppressive; and the privateers fell off in number as well as in hardihood. As a sort of compensation for this, the royal navy rose into more prominence than it had before enjoyed. Between 1603 and 1618 James I. had added to the latter no less than seventeen ships, one of them of 1400 tons.[2] The profligacy of the later Stuarts, however, and their necessity for money in the midst of their domestic broils with Parliament, led them frequently to use for private purposes the appropriations destined for the navy; the latter, therefore, enjoyed but a precarious prestige, which was sadly interrupted when Ruyter sailed up the Thames in 1667 and destroyed a great deal of English shipping, including several men-of-war.[3] On the other hand, two years before, the English had captured the entire Bordeaux fleet of the Dutch, consisting of 130 sail, and Sir Thomas Allen had dispersed a fleet of forty Dutch vessels

trated by the following somewhat ludicrous incident: In 1605 Sir William Monson, with a vessel of the royal navy, encountered two Dutch ships in the Channel, which saluted his "in the usual way; but, by way of putting a disgrace upon her, *the trumpeter blurred with his trumpet, which is held a scorn at sea*" (Southey, *Lives*, etc., V., 115). For this offence the Dutch captains were compelled to come on board Monson's vessel and apologize, besides agreeing to punish the trumpeter; the insult they attributed to the latter's "lewdness."

[1] In 1667 the Lord High Admiral, brother of the king, although a man of some experience and perfectly able to serve, "remained safe at home and by virtue of his post . . . took to himself a large share of the prizes which were made; besides which the parliament voted him a handsome present." *Hervey, Hist. R. N.*, II., 241.

[2] The Prince Royal.

[3] The indifference of Charles II. to the naval decline during his reign, and particularly to the success of Ruyter, is caustically described by Lavisse and Rambaud in their *Histoire Générale du IVme Siècle à nos Jours*, vol. 6, chapter on the Restoration: "On se demande où est le roi . . . On répond qu'il donne la chasse à un papillon avec une serviette chez Lady Castlemaine."

coming home richly laden from Smyrna. The Peace of Breda in 1667 left New York with the English; but the British Navigation Act was altered in a very material particular to the advantage of the Dutch.¹

Privateering did not revive to any great extent under William and Mary. The days of the government's conniving at piracy were past, and in 1694 Governor John Easton of the colony of Rhode Island is recorded as having refused a privateer's commission to one Thomas Tew, on account of his past history.² On the other hand, the French privateers had been very active ever since the ministry of Colbert; these were the days of Jean Bart, Duguay-Trouin, and the filibusters; and during the war immediately preceding the Peace of Ryswick, 4200 English vessels fell a prey to them. The total loss to English merchants is estimated at £30,000,-000.³ Such was the situation when Anne ascended the throne in 1702 and the war of the Spanish succession began.

3

From the Prize Act of Anne (1708) to the First Armed Neutrality (1780).

The experience of the seventeenth century had shown that, except where the hostile commerce was prodigiously rich, privateering would not flourish under the existing prize law. The 4 and 5 William and Mary, c. 25,⁴ had reserved to the crown only one-fifth of all prizes taken by private individuals; yet even under this and the act of March, 1702, mari-

¹ So as to permit the importation into England, in Dutch bottoms, of the produce of the Rhenish States.
² W. P. Sheffield, *Privateersmen of Newport*, Appendix, note 2.
³ Nys, *La Guerre Maritime*, p. 29; Cauchy, *Du Respect de la propriété privée*, etc., p. 37.
⁴ Cf. Robinson, *Collectanea Maritima* (1801), p. 193 n.

time enterprise did not seem to revive. Heroic measures were necessary to restore the institution which had done so much for Elizabeth and for Henry VIII.; and on March 26, 1708, a new prize act,[1] passed by Parliament, was approved by the queen. This act is a crucial point in the history of English privateering. It marks the close of the period of decline and the opening of the period of greatest activity. It provided, briefly, for the transfer of the entire interest in the prize to the privateer,[2] and for an additional sum by way of bounty, based on the number of men on board the captured ship at the commencement of the action.[3] It was a definite change of policy on the part of the British government. From this time the government ceases to expect any direct benefit from privateering, and sanctions it only for the indirect benefit which it hopes to derive from the injury to the enemy and the enrichment of its own subjects.

Some time, however, was necessary before the effects of the new system could be felt by a generation of sailors long discouraged from great enterprises; and the Peace of Utrecht was concluded without much help from private adventurers. In 1739 war broke out with Spain, and in spite of a substantial re-enactment of the act of 1708 (April, 1740), the records of the years 1739–1741 show only thirty prizes taken by individuals as against 259 taken by the regular navy.[4]

[1] An Act for the better securing the Trade of this Kingdom by Cruisers and Convoys, and for the Encouragement of Cruisers, 6 Anne, c. 13.

[2] " . . . That from and after the 26th of March, 1708, if any ship or ships of war, privateer, merchant ship or other vessel shall be taken as prize in any of her Majesty's Courts of Admiralty, the flag-officer or officers, commander or commanders, and other officers, seamen and others who shall be actually on board such ship or ships of war or privateers, shall after such condemnation have the sole interest and property in such prize or prizes."

[3] § VIII. (£5 for each man). Compare the French system of bounties, *infra*, based on guns instead of men.

[4] These and the other figures in this subdivision are those given by Leeder, *Die Englische Kaperei und die Thätigkeit der Admiralitätsgerichte* (Berlin, 1881).

And in March, 1744, when the war with France began, the English adventurers were not quite holding their own against the Spanish. A royal proclamation in May offered free pardon to certain minor criminals under sentence or in jail awaiting trial, who should consent to serve on board a ship of war or privateer. In addition to the smugglers and outlaws thus turned loose upon the world as representatives of the King of England, the mercantile circles began at last to awake to the advantages offered them by the new prize law. In 1744 the merchants of London alone equipped thirty-nine privateers, and those of Bristol eighteen; by the close of the next year 190 were on the seas. Out of 440 French and Spanish prizes taken during these years, 200 were taken by privateers. On the other hand, great damage was done to English shipping by the French and the Spaniards, and it became slowly and painfully apparent to the British government that the real gainers by the war were the Dutch, into whose hands, as neutrals, the entire colonial trade of the French and Spanish had fallen. Making but little stir, the Dutch were quietly regaining the commercial supremacy of which they had been robbed by the English in the preceding century; with the result that their complaints of the outrages of English privateers were received with deaf ears by George II. and his Privy Council. This fact was quickly observed by the privateers, whose excesses increased daily. The order of Parliament that "whatsoever vessel shall be met withal transporting any soldiers, arms, powder, ammunition, or *other contraband goods*" was stretched *ad libitum* by each individual privateer, there being no limit to the number of things which the admiralty courts might decide to call "contraband."[1] At any rate, it scarcely ever

[1] The subsisting treaties between England and several neutral powers defined contraband precisely, and that of 1674 with Holland provided Free Ships, Free Goods. Nevertheless, privateers constantly brought in Spanish goods in Dutch

did any harm to bring them in, for the admiralty courts, recognizing the national policy to harass neutral commerce, were almost sure to find some technical ground on which to tax the neutral master with costs, even if the vessel and cargo were restored.[1] Moreover the damage done to neutrals by the delay necessary for putting in motion the ponderous machinery of the admiralty, was incalculable. The Danish ship *Junge Benjamin* was detained six and a half months; out of eighteen Prussian ships taken without any probable cause, three were detained for periods ranging from eight to ten months, and one for thirteen months, and the Swedish ships *Carlshaven* and *Prinz Gustav* were released only after a detention of twelve and fifteen months, respectively.

The Dutch, although their losses during the war amounted to nearly £1,300,000, found themselves unable to do anything but threaten; and they remained the butt of the privateers till the peace in 1748. With Prussia, however, the question was more serious. The case of Captain Bugdahl[2]

bottoms, and a new kind of "contraband" was invented in order that they might be condemned.

[1] ". . . so sorgte doch die Thätigkeit des englischen Admiralitätsgerichts, dass die Kaptoren wenigstens keinen Schaden durch Kostenersatz litten, und daher bis zum Ende des Krieges das mühelose Aufbringen der neutralen Schiffe fortsetzten."—(Leeder, p. 25). Out of 14 Dutch ships and cargoes wholly or partially restored in 1748, costs and damages (£2801) were awarded to only one.

[2] See Bugdahl's report, Leeder, 20, 21. On May 5 he left Bordeaux; on the 7th he was boarded by an English privateer, which, after looking at his papers, tried to induce him to say that some of the goods on board were French (*habe er ihn sehr karessiert doch zu sagen, ob nicht französische Güter an Bord seien*); when he denied this, they fell without more ado to plundering him, taking his maps, charts, etc., maltreating him and his crew, and piercing holes in the wine-casks so that the wine ran out upon the deck. Finally, after an unsuccessful attempt to burn the ship, they left him. Next day about dusk came two other privateers, one of which boarded him, and, being shown his papers, carried them off, whereupon the other privateer boarded, and not finding any papers sent him into Liverpool!

had aroused the ire of the great Frederick, and, less impotent than the Dutch, he proceeded to retaliate by sequestrating the Silesian loan and applying the interest thereon to the indemnification of the outraged Prussian merchants. So matters stood when the Peace of Aix-la-Chapelle was signed in 1748.

Disputes as to boundaries in America, and as to the ownership of some of the Caribbean islands, provoked, as between England and France, the Seven Years' War in 1756. By a strange combination of circumstances Prussia was obliged to forget the past and form a coalition with England; and Austria, in the hope of recovering Silesia, as well as for the purpose of strengthening the Netherlands, united herself with France. Long before the declarations of war, English privateers, scenting booty as vultures scent carrion, had covered the seas, and, taking the fighting in America as an excuse, had fallen upon great numbers of French merchantmen. It is estimated that they took, "*dans cette première surprise*,"[1] more than 300 vessels and nearly 10,000 peaceful sailors.

In the following year (1757) privateering became a craze the like of which had never been seen in England. The Duchess of Nottingham, with some ladies of the court, equipped three large vessels; companies were formed all over Great Britain and Ireland for the purpose of carrying on the trade of plundering the French; the fishermen of Jersey and the Channel islands left their nets and patrolled the coasts in little boats, armed only with clubs, knives and pistols. Heretofore, the average strength of the English privateers had been something like 20 guns and 120 to 150 men; now we find "privateers" with three and four guns, and even no guns at all, stopping large neutral vessels and exercising the right of visitation and search. The result is

[1] Anquetil, *Motifs des Guerres*, p. 323. See also Doneaud, *Hist. de la Marine Française*, ch. iv.

forcibly illustrated by the experience of the *Jonge Katharina*, a Dutch ship which sailed from Amsterdam in April, 1757, bound for San Sebastian:

On April 20 she was stopped by a fishing-boat off Dover; of nine men in the boat seven came on board and plundered. On the same day another fishing-smack, containing twelve men, came alongside, and *all twelve* came on board and plundered. A mile further on she encountered a third, armed with clubs and pistols; the crew of this one broke a great deal of stuff, besides stealing after the fashion of the others. At midnight she was boarded again, but it was too dark to see what was stolen *(man konnte aber in der Nacht nicht sehen, was sie mitnahmen*[1]*)*. Next day early came a fifth little privateer, which loaded itself with goods, and later a sixth, which demanded gold from the Dutch captain. At noon came two together, ten men in each, and committed various thefts. Still later another came in sight, this time a large one; the searching boat which it sent out, however, was filled with goods from the unfortunate Dutchman, and soon afterwards the same privateer sent out another boat which "loaded itself to the gunwales." On the 27th came a tenth and last, which really did no damage of any kind *(ohne etwas zu beschädigen)*. It is not unlikely, indeed, that by this time there was nothing left on the *Jonge Katharina* to damage.[2] Nor was this a solitary instance. A list of 33 ships wrongfully plundered by privateers was

---

[1] Leeder, *Die Englische Kaperei*, p. 34.

[2] The account is taken from Leeder's condensed translation of the *Verklaring van't Schip de Jonge Katharina* (*Die Englische Kaperei*, p. 34). Other cases almost as bad were those of the *Katharina Maria, Princess Karolina, Gertruida, Juliana, Pieter*. From the *Verklaring van't Schip de Goode Resolutie*, we find that it was robbed by a small privateer and taken into Guernsey, where, *although there was no admiralty court*, it was detained seven months. It was then released without trial, "aber kaum auf dem Meere von einem anderen Kaper geplündert."

presented on Nov. 11, 1757, to the Dutch ambassador at London; on July 27, 1758, a list of 56 cases was submitted by the merchants of Amsterdam to their High Mightinesses, and Leeder mentions still a third list of 100 cases.¹

The great master-stroke of English maritime policy, however, was what has since been known as the "Rule" of the war of 1756, which was announced to foreign powers for the first time in 1758, by the English ambassador at the Hague. According to that rule, the Dutch and other neutrals were prohibited from carrying on any trade, directly or indirectly, with the French colonies, which trade was not guaranteed to them in time of peace.² This arbitrary innovation, which was received with the utmost joy and enforced unsparingly by the privateers, was a death-blow to the Dutch commerce, which had been growing rich on the French colonial trade for many years. Other neutrals suffered in less degree. In 1757, before the proclamation of the rule, the English privateers had brought in for adjudication 153 French and 35 neutral vessels.³ In 1758, after its proclamation, they brought in 128 French and 130 neutrals.⁴ And this does not include the captures of the public vessels of war, which from seven neutral ships in 1757 rose to 33 in 1758.

But now, in addition to the complaints and reprisals of Spain and other neutral powers more able to resent injury than the Dutch, the protests of the English insurers became so alarming that the government was obliged to rouse itself

---

¹ " Es war im Laufe eines Jahres," says he (p. 37), " aus der englischen Kaperei in Europa eine Piraterie geworden . . . ; damals waren es die Admiralitätsgerichte gewesen, welche den Neutralen den Hauptschaden zufügten; jetzt teilten sich Gerichte, Kaper und Piraten in diese Aufgabe."

² *Annual Register*, 1758.

³ 17 Dutch, 9 Swedish, 4 Spanish, 3 Danish, 2 Hanseatic.

⁴ 101 Dutch, 10 Spanish, 11 Swedish, 4 Danish, 2 Hanseatic, 2 Portuguese.

from its policy of inactivity. A great deal of the loss was falling on English shoulders, and prudence and economy both suggested the advisability of reform. Moreover, the Dutch were already ruined, and the principal motive for secretly encouraging piracies had therefore disappeared. The 32 Geo. 2, c. 25,[1] provided that no privateer commission should be granted for the future unless the ship applying for it should be "of the burthen of a hundred tons, and carry ten carriage guns, being three-pounders, and forty men at the least," except in the discretion of the lords of the Admiralty and upon proper security; and all existing commissions to vessels under the required strength were revoked (Section XVII). Further, privateers agreeing for the ransom of neutral ships without bringing them into port were to be deemed guilty of piracy (Section XII). The effect of this act was, of course, to sweep away the little fishermen-privateers which infested the Channel, and to produce a marked improvement in the conduct of the larger ones. Some twenty-five privateer captains were tried for piracy under its provisions, for ransoming neutral vessels or cruising without a commission; and from June, 1759, till the Peace of Paris (1763), the neutral complaints fell off gradually in number and the London insurers thrived. The Peace of Paris demonstrated forcibly how little influence privateering usually exercises on the result of a war; the losses of the English shipping were more than double those of the French, yet the treaty of peace was the most disgraceful, perhaps, that France ever signed. The English captures at sea had far less to do with the treaty than Madame de Pompadour.

Whatever its causes, however, the Peace of Paris was a triumph of English maritime policy and a confirmation of

[1] An Act for the Encouragement of Seamen and the Prevention of Piracies by Private Ships of War.

English sea-despotism.[1] But, under the vigorous administration of Louis XVI., the French navy increased with rapid strides, and the national desire to renew hostilities with England became impossible to restrain after the American Revolution assumed serious proportions. The Franco-American alliance of 1778 was followed by the Franco-Spanish alliance of 1779, the Family Compact and the possibility of recovering Gibraltar being the arguments which Vergennes had used to procure the latter. The great, oppressive maritime system of Great Britain was revived, the Rule of 1756 reestablished, and privateers, better equipped than ever before,[2] were sent out with commissions against the three powers. To all appearances the sickening proceedings of the Seven Years' War were about to be repeated, when two outrages committed by British cruisers upon Russian commerce[3] aroused the ire of the latter power, and led to Catharine II's declaration of the 26th of February, 1780.[4] This famous

---

[1] Jacobsen (*Seerecht der Engländer und Franzosen*, Hamburg, 1803), says mildly of this despotism, that neutrals had naturally to pay "ein unerhörtes und schmerzhaftes Lehrgeld zu einer Zeit, wo die Engländer über ihr jetziges System noch selbst nur sagen konnten, *docendo discimus*, indem sie noch selbst nicht wussten, wo sie hinaus wollten" (I., 556). It seems more than likely, however, that if the nation generally was kept in ignorance, the men who controlled the maritime policy of Great Britain knew very well "wo sie hinaus wollten."

[2] See James, *Naval History*, I., 59. In 1779 the "smasher" gun, or carronade, had not yet been adopted in the royal navy, but many privateers were equipped with them.

[3] Two Riga vessels, *Der Emmanuel* and *Der Junge Prinz*, hemp and flax, for Bordeaux and Nantes respectively, were captured and sent into England, where, "allen Vorstellungen des russischen Generalconsuls in London zum Trotz," they were detained *a year*. Bergbohm, *Die Bewaffnete Neutralität*, p. 116.

[4] More appropriately, Count Panin's declaration. It is well known that Catharine II. was herself a cordial friend of the English, and was simply tricked into the armed neutrality by Panin, who induced her to believe that it would be most galling to Spain. The Spanish seizure of two Russian vessels carrying corn to Gibraltar, urged the minister, should be resented, and resented in a way which should enable Russia to pose as the protector of neutral rights against the world. So

document, which declared that all neutral vessels might, of right, navigate freely from port to port and along the coasts of nations at war; which laid down the principle Free Ships Free Goods, and defined contraband so as to exclude materials of naval construction, besides denouncing as invalid all "paper" or ineffective blockades, was hailed with joy by all the belligerent powers except Great Britain. By a convention, signed at Copenhagen on the 9th of July, Denmark adopted the Russian declaration and agreed to assist in its enforcement, if necessary, by war; Sweden acceded to this convention on the 9th of September; and the three great northern powers, by mutual consent, declared the Baltic closed to the belligerents. Austria acceded to the "Armed Neutrality" Oct. 9, 1781; Portugal, July 13, 1782; and the two Sicilies, Feb. 10, 1783. Holland also acceded, before she became involved in the war; and the United States, in its eagerness to acquiesce in the principles of the Russian declaration, declared an intention to "accede" as early as April 7, 1781, oblivious of the fact that a belligerent power could not technically become a member of a neutral alliance.

This portentous league, which "continued to hang as a dark cloud constantly menacing the safety of the British empire until the peace of 1783,"[1] destroyed, for the time, the great

blind was the Czarina to the consequences of the declaration, that she is recorded as saying confidentially to Sir James Harris, the English minister at St. Petersburg, that she would shortly issue a manifesto which would be most acceptable to England. In Harris' despatch to Lord Stormont, of the 24th of December, 1780, he reports the following conversation with the empress (*Cf.*, Fauchille, *La Dip. Française*, p. 589):

"HARRIS: Il [Panin] est déjà lui-même dans une intelligence parfaite avec le cabinet de Versailles.

"L'IMPÉRATRICE (*piquée*): Ne croyez pas que cela signifie quelque chose; je connais à fond M. Panin; ses intrigues ne font plus rien sur moi; je ne suis pas un enfant; personne ne m'empêche de faire ce que je veux, je vois clair."

[1] Wheaton, *History of the Law of Nations*, p. 303.

British scheme of maritime despotism. "In 1781 and 1782," says Fauchille,[1] "secret instructions were issued to the English privateers to moderate their zeal (*pour tempérer leur zèle*)." The neutral flag protecting hostile goods, and the other powers being determined to prevent the enforcement of the Rule of 1756, there was little booty left for the adventurers, and in the last three years of the war they fell off greatly in number. The excesses of the Seven Years' War had not helped to procure the advantageous Peace of Paris; they had helped to produce the exceedingly anti-English sentiment which raised the world in arms against England in 1780, and compelled her ultimately to accept the disadvantageous Peace of Versailles.

4

From the First Armed Neutrality to the Declaration of Paris (1856)

How far the maritime pretensions of England have depended upon the maritime condition of France must already have been apparent. The weakness of the French marine under Louis XV. was the occasion for the invention of the Rule of 1756; the strength of the French marine under Louis XVI., together with its Russian support, caused the abandonment of that rule in 1780.

When the war of 1793 began, the French navy was broken up and demoralized; the revolution had carried away its great commanders; even D'Estaing was about to fall under the guillotine; and the time, therefore, seemed ripe for a revival of English domination. The Anglo-Russian treaty of March 25, 1793, engaged both parties to do all in their power, "on this occasion of common concern to every civilized state," to prevent other powers from giving, "in consequence of their

---

[1] Fauchille, *La Diplomatie Française et la Ligue des Neutres*, p. 580.

neutrality," any protection to French property or commerce.[1] Similar provisions are found in the Spanish, Prussian and Austrian treaties with Great Britain of May 25, July 14 and August 30, respectively. Stringent provisions were made for starving France into submission, under the ingenious pretext of treating provisions as contraband.[2] The Convention answered by the decree of the 9th of May, ordering the pre-emption of all provisions bound for an English or other hostile port. An Order in Council then issued (Nov. 6, 1793),[3] *reviving the rule of 1756*, and as Russia was then allied with England, the northern powers interposed no objection. Of course the neutral flag was not recognized as protecting French goods, even Russia, in view of the importance of the occasion, departing from her former policy in this regard. The English privateers, therefore, appeared in great numbers, attracted by the wide range of booty which the government offered them.[4] They were, it will be seen,

---

[1] *Amer. State Papers, For. Rel.*, III., p. 263.

[2] See Hall, *Int. Law*, ch. on Contraband. It was not till the 8th of June, 1793, that British privateers were formally instructed to "detain all vessels laden with corn, flour, meal," etc. But the privateers had begun to do so on their own responsibility before the French decree of the 9th May. France must not be judged too harshly for that decree. To-day, with plenty of corn in our granaries, we can hardly appreciate the terrible condition of France in 1793, nor the excuses which the Comité du Salut Public had for its remark, "There is no immorality in ruining those who starve us."

[3] *Am. State Papers, For. Rel.*, III., p. 264.

[4] The 33 Geo. 3, c. 66, An Act for the Encouragement of Seamen, and for the better and more effectually manning His Majesty's Navy, is in some respects a model privateer act. Sec. IX. provides that the owner of any vessel registered under the 26 Geo. 3, whom the Lord High Admiral, or the Commissioners, etc., shall deem fitly qualified, may obtain a commission or "letters of marque and reprizal" and enjoy the whole benefit of the prizes taken. Sec. XIV. provides for security "such as hath been usual in such cases." Sec. XV. requires that applications shall be in writing, and contain description of ship, etc. Sec. XXI. provides that offences on board privateers shall be punished as if committed on board ships of war.

entitled to seize: (1) French vessels, (2) neutral vessels
laden wholly or in part with French merchandise, (3) neutral vessels laden with provisions bound for France, (4) neutral vessels laden with contraband for France, (5) neutral
vessels laden with French colonial produce. In addition, the
system of paper blockades was revived, and this became the
most oppressive, perhaps, of all the maritime pretensions of
Great Britain, particularly to Americans. The practice was
to issue a circular notification of blockade, announcing that
"the King has judged it expedient" to institute one, and
that *therefore* it must be considered as existing.[1] As a
matter of fact it might be several weeks afterwards before any English squadron approached the town or harbor
declared blockaded. Under these arbitrary rules American
commerce suffered heavily. The list of British captures
during the year 1796[2] and the list of captured vessels
belonging to the Messrs. Smith of Baltimore, deposited
in the Department of State June 17, 1797, contained matter
well calculated to inflame the American mind against England. The same old principle of seizing everything and
relying on the court of admiralty to allow at least costs,
seems to be present; else how explain the capture of vessels
laden with flour and coffee on their way to Baltimore;[3] of
the schooner *Lively*, on the sole pretext that she carried ten
casks of nails;[4] of the brig *Jefferson*, because her owner, Mr.
Longchamp, "had been in France in the last three years"
and had a brother who was a conscript in the French ser-

---

[1] See Lord Harrowby's Circular of Aug. 9, 1804 (Fécamp) and Lord Grenville's of March 22, 1799 (all ports of Holland).

[2] *Am. State Papers, For. Rel.*, II., 30.

[3] See the cases (in the Smith's list) of the *Sidney*, the *Fell's Point*, the *Fanny*, and the *Sally*.

[4] Which, by the way, were condemned. *Am. St. Papers, For. Rel.*, II., 30.

vice;[1] or the schooner *St. Patrick*, direct from Curaçao to an American port, and carrying only American property, notwithstanding which she was decreed to pay costs on the ground that the captor had had "probable cause." The *Susanna*, of Charleston, with sugar, to Cadiz, was captured while trying to ascertain whether Cadiz was blockaded (for under the British practice it was impossible to discover except by asking), and tried and condemned in Gibraltar while she, with all her crew, was at Lisbon.[2] Mr. Fitzsimons, in a letter of February 17, 1801, on behalf of the Philadelphia Chamber of Commerce to the Secretary of the Navy,[3] declared that without convoys all trade to Cuba would have to be abandoned. Premiums to Havana rose twenty per cent. in a few days. "Not one in ten vessels," wrote Mr. Fitzsimons, "can escape; from New Providence alone there are above forty privateers who subsist principally by the plunder of the Americans." "The enforcement of the Rule of 1756," he continued, "was the more mortifying, as they themselves ship the goods of which they plunder the Americans to the countries to which they do not permit us to carry them." Perhaps, however, the most remarkable case of outrage before the Peace of Amiens was the capture of the *Crocodile*, Curaçao to New York, carrying only Dutch and American property: "The captors, immediately on the capture, *made a privateer of the Crocodile and sent her on a cruise*."[4]

Russia, once more neutral, began to be restive under this revival of British aggression. Not only did she refuse to

---

[1] Representation of the Merchants of Norfolk. *Am. St. Papers, For. Rel.*, II., 764.
[2] "... without even the captain being present." U. S. Consul at Gibraltar to Secretary of State, Nov. 19, 1800.
[3] *Am. State Papers, For. Rel.*, II., 347.
[4] *Am. State Papers, For. Rel.*, II., 345.

acknowledge the Rule of 1756, but she returned to her ancient dogma, Free Ships Free Goods, and moreover contended for the immunity of convoyed vessels from visitation and search. The case of the Danish convoy, $\frac{14}{25}$th July, 1800, which the English stopped and searched by force, precipitated matters and led to the Second Armed Neutrality. On the 16th of December, 1800, there was signed by Russia and Sweden a convention,[1] to which Prussia and Denmark afterwards acceded, providing for a renewal of the principles of the old Armed Neutrality and for the immunity of convoyed vessels. Article III. also provided that probable cause should be necessary for capture, and that there should be no unnecessary delay in the matter of trial—thus introducing a sort of *habeas corpus* principle into maritime law.

The announcement of the Russo-Swedish alliance was followed by an Order in Council directing an embargo on Russian and Swedish vessels (Jan. 14, 1801). Lord Grenville declared that "the maritime code of 1780, now sought to be revived, was an innovation highly injurious to the dearest interests of Great Britain."[2] Hostilities followed, during which the emperor Paul died; and though the Anglo-Russian convention of June 17, 1801, is on its face a compromise, it was really a triumph of Russian policy and a severe check to Great Britain. Russia gave up Free Ships Free Goods, but her adversary abandoned the Rule of 1756 (art. III. §§ 1, 2) and conceded the immunity of convoyed vessels from search by privateers (art. IV. § 1).

The brief Peace of Amiens gave way in 1803 to the most

---

[1] This convention refers to the First Armed Neutrality as the system "suivi avec tant de succès pendant la dernière guerre d'Amérique," and the Czar Paul, in his declaration of Aug. 15, says of it enthusiastically: "Chacune [of the signatory powers] en recueillit des avantages sans nombre."

[2] Wheaton, *History of the Law of Nations*, p. 400.

violent and lawless period of war, and especially maritime war, that the modern world has ever seen. During this period we are dealing no longer with questions of international law. That, with all other law, was laid upon the shelf, and its retirement justified by the magic word, Reprisal! From 1803 to 1806, the British pretensions, not yet recovered from the shock of the Second Armed Neutrality, were, indeed, asserted gradually and with care. The Rule of 1756, in accordance with a report of the king's advocate of March 16, 1801,[1] was enforced only against *direct* trade from the colony to the mother country; and under a decision of the High Court of Admiralty the landing of the goods and the payment of duties in the neutral country was held to break the continuity of the voyage and render the trade indirect. This interpretation of the rule, sent by Lord Hawkesbury to Mr. King in 1801, and published, at Mr. King's suggestion, in all the American newspapers, was faithfully followed until the summer of 1805. Then, however, "when a large amount of American property was afloat, undeniably entitled to the protection of the above rule, and committed to the high seas under an implicit reliance upon a strict adherence to it, the rule was suddenly abandoned, and British cruisers fell upon this trade"[2] under a new decision that the *intention* of the importer of colonial produce to export the produce to the mother country constituted the trade in such produce a direct trade.[3] Sir Evan Nepean's assurance[4] (Jan. 5, 1804) that Commodore Hood was instructed not to treat any blockade of Martinique or Guadalupe as existing "unless in respect of particular parts actually invested," did not prevent the

[1] *British and For. State Papers*, I., 1204.
[2] Messrs. Monroe and Pinckney to Lords Holland and Auckland, Aug. 20, 1806.
[3] *Cf.* Memorial of Merchants of New York, Dec. 28, 1805, *Am. St. P., For. Rel.*, II., 737.
[4] Sir E. Nepean to Mr. Hammond, *British and For. State Papers*, I., 1207.

seizure of the schooner *Nancy* and other vessels on the theory of a paper blockade;[1] and the indefensible British method of search, which consisted in compelling the vessel visited to *send her papers in her own boat* to the privateer, instead of leaving the burden with the searchers,[2] was practised with unabated frequency. The masterly inactivity of the admiralty courts in this and the preceding period is forcibly illustrated by the case of Ira Allen. Mr. Allen, sent to Europe by the governor of Vermont to procure arms for his militia, was induced, by the difference in price, to buy the arms in a French market rather. than an English one. In 1796, while returning with his purchase, he was taken into England by a 74-gun cruiser, and, in the following year, the cargo was condemned, Mariott, J., "suggesting that it was intended to arm the rebels of Ireland." On appeal, the vessel was detained under the form of restoration with bail "for more evidence;" and it was not actually restored until the bail became bankrupt, which was seven years afterwards (1804).[3] Incidentally it is to be noted in connection with the case that *no more evidence was ever adduced;* so that if there was enough for restoration in 1804, there must have been enough in 1797.

All of these practices, however, were moderation itself, in comparison with the series of acts which began in 1806. Early in that year (May 16) the numerous little blockades which the British had instituted on the northern coast of France and the low countries, were consolidated, and one general blockade from the river Elbe to the port of Brest was announced.[4] Napoleon, master of Prussia, seized the

[1] *Am. State Papers, For. Rel.*, II., 765.
[2] Report of the Secretary of State (Madison), Jan. 25, 1806. *Am. St. Papers, For. Rel.*, II., 728.
[3] *Am. State Papers, For. Rel.*, II.
[4] *British and Forign State Papers*, I., 1512.

opportunity to issue his famous Berlin decree (Nov. 21), declaring the British Isles "*en état de blocus,*" and forbidding neutrals to have any commerce or intercourse with them.[1] Thereupon (Jan. 7, 1807), an Order in Council issued, which, after reciting that France had proclaimed a blockade of Great Britain "at a time when the fleets of France and her allies are themselves confined within their own ports by the superior valor and discipline of the British navy," forbade neutrals to trade from one port to another in France.[2] This, however, was found inadequate, and one of the three Orders in Council of Nov. 11, 1807,[3] provided that "all ports in Europe from which the British flag is excluded, shall be subject to the same restrictions as if the same were actually blockaded by His Majesty's naval forces." The same Order in Council directed vessels of war and privateers to make prize of neutrals complying with the French requirement of carrying "certificates of origin" to show that their cargoes were not English; and certain neutral vessels were to be obliged to "proceed to some port or place in the United Kingdom or to Gibraltar or Malta," and be subjected to certain exactions. Another Order in Council of the same date declared that vessels belonging to French subjects at the beginning of the war should continue subject to seizure till the end, regardless of all transfers or pledges to neutrals; in other words, once French, always French.[4] Napoleon, on the 17th of December, 1807, issued his Milan decree, declaring that the French would make prize of any vessel "submitting" to the Orders

---

[1] *Cf.* Arts. 1 and 2. The preamble reviews 'the British practice of declaring blockaded places "devant lesquelles elle n'a pas même un seul bâtiment de guerre," and of applying the law of blockade not only to fortified towns, but to the mouths of rivers and generally "des côtes entières." This conduct the Emperor of the French stigmatizes as "digne des premiers âges de la barbarie."

[2] *British and For. State Papers,* VIII., 468.   [3] *Ibid.,* 491.   [4] *Id.,* I., 1512.

in Council of the 11th November,[1] and continuing the imaginary blockade of the British Isles. By this time the sea had become no place for neutrals. It was a strife between Titans, and the onlookers must keep out of the arena. Both England and France were unable, even if willing, to control the hordes of desperate privateers and quasi-privateers who were nominally subject to them. During the Peninsular war, on account of the difficulty of feeding the army, it was customary to issue licenses to certain American vessels, exempting them from seizure on any ground by British cruisers, in consideration of their supplying provisions; and it is on record that "the captain of a Scotch merchant vessel, engaged in the same trade, and having no letter of marque, had the piratical insolence to seize, in the very mouth of the Tagus, and under the Portuguese batteries, an American vessel sailing under the license of Mr. Foster, and to carry her into Greenock, thus violating at once the license of the English minister, the independence of Portugal, and the general law of nations."[2]

It is unnecessary here to go into the complicated question as to whether the decrees of Berlin and Milan were ever really repealed. It is practically certain, at any rate, that the revocation of the British Orders in Council, on the 23d of June, 1812, five days after the Congress of the United States had declared war, was not in consequence of, or in any way connected with, the French decree of April 28, 1811, purporting to effect that repeal.[3] The revocation of the Orders in

[1] Art. I. Any vessel which " se sera soumis à un voyage en Angleterre, on aura payé une imposition quelconque au Gouvernement Anglais, est par cela seul déclaré dénationalisé," etc. The preamble sets forth that this is absolutely necessary, because if, " par une faiblesse inexcusable, on laissait passer en principe et consacrer par l'usage une pareille tyrannie, les Anglais en prendraient acte pour l'établir en droit," etc.

[2] *Napier's History of the Peninsular War*, IV., 30.

[3] " The real cause of the revocation," wrote Mr. Russell to Mr. Monroe, June

Council was the result of economic considerations purely, and not of any desire on the part of the British government to return to the paths of law and order. Every one knows the effect of the American war upon British maritime policy. The Treaty of Ghent is the bow of a world's champion to a newly-discovered equal. Between, though not in its lines, we read Great Britain's confession that the day of marine despotism is over; that the policy of marine despotism can never be revived. For there cannot be two despots.

During the American war every effort was made to recede from the high-handed position previously assumed, with as little shock as possible. The blockades were raised from each port as soon as the power of France was driven back sufficiently to afford the slightest excuse for so doing. The ports of the Netherlands were declared open December 13, 1813; Triest and Dalmatia were relieved on the same day; and on January 14, 1814, many ports of France itself were proclaimed free.[1] The check at the hands of the United States was compensated for by the victory over France; the British despotism-system imparted to its own death a sort of *éclat* by dragging with it in still more hopeless ruin the "Continental System" of Napoleon.

The fall of the latter marks the close of the history of English privateers. Though they had done nothing to promote the peace, though they had succeeded only in injuring neutrals and causing the name of England to be execrated throughout the earth, they were so essential a part of the English system that the prince regent revived them as a

---

30, 1812 (*Am. St. Papers, For. Rel.*, III., 615), "is the measures of our government," *i. e.*, the embargo of December, 1807, to March, 1809, and the non-intercourse act of May, 1810, which produced acute suffering in England. See also the elaborate argument of the Secretary of State, in his report of July 12, 1813 (*Am. St. Papers, For. Rel.*, III., 609).

[1] *Brit. and For. State Papers*, I., 1267

matter of course during the Hundred Days.[1] But in the long interval of peace from 1815 to the Crimean war, there was ample time for the digestion of facts with regard to this institution, and in consequence, its popularity decidedly declined. Its inhumanity, its invariable effect of producing complications with neutrals, and above all its ineffectiveness, made it no fit weapon to use against Russia in 1854, and both France and England refused to issue "letters of mark."[2] Indeed, the Russian commerce was so small, and the British regular navy so powerful, that privateers would have been superfluous. The regular navy captured 205 Russian vessels (all, except one, unarmed); 136 were wholly condemned.[3]

[1] Order in Council, June 21, 1815, *British and For. State Papers*, II., 1044.

[2] *Cf.* Queen's Procl., Mar. 28, 1854, *Br. and For. State Papers*, XLVI., 36.

[3] Return of the Names and Number of Russian vessels captured, etc., ordered by the House of Commons to be printed, July 29, 1856.

CHAPTER II

PRIVATEERING IN FRANCE

I

The French Marine before Colbert

"*La marine en France,*" says Doneaud,[1] "*est un élément de puissance, mais non pas la puissance même du pays, comme en Angleterre.*" Always a naval power of the first class, France has never been the chief of naval powers, nor, with the exception of a few years under Louis XVI., does she seem ever to have had any ambition to be such. There have been no "sailor kings" in France. Her monarchs have almost invariably been content with bare equality upon the sea; and the dream of reviving the empire of Charles the Great has been to them what that of maritime supremacy was to England. The motives for the employment of privateers in France and England have not therefore been altogether identical. To cripple the enemy by cutting him off from his colonies and generally destroying his trade is a purpose which was common to both; but to direct the excesses of private adventurers against neutrals, who, if allowed to escape unscathed, might become commercial rivals, was a policy which France, in the absence of any wish to establish a maritime despotism, never adopted. Privateers were used in England as something auxiliary to the royal navy; in France very often because there was nothing else to use. In early times, when there was no regular navy, and in later

---

[1] *Hist. de la Marine Française,* Preface.

times, when the regular navy was now and again driven off the seas by the English, it was a question of commissioning private individuals, or of allowing the French flag to disappear from the ocean altogether. In this position Louis XIV. found himself after the battle of La Hogue, and Napoleon after Aboukir and Trafalgar.

Before the royal marine became permanent under Colbert, the kings of France, like those of England, relied for their maritime operations upon impromptu navies raised by the impressment or hiring of merchant vessels. In France there was nothing analogous to the Cinque Ports, and the method of raising the contributions varied with the exigencies of each particular war. The decentralized state of the country, moreover, made it possible for private adventure to develop an amount of importance and independence which would have been impossible in England under the strong and jealous Anglo-Norman kingship. The most remarkable illustration of this tendency to independence is the case of Ango of Dieppe in 1525. The Portuguese having seized one of his ships and denied him redress, Ango, at his own cost, fitted out seventeen armed vessels with which, in due form, he blockaded the Tagus.[1] Francis I, in answer to the Portuguese complaints, is said to have remarked, "*Messieurs, ce n'est pas moi qui fais la guerre; allez trouver Ango, et arrangez-vous avec lui.*"[2] A certain Vandervelde is said to have been created Chevalier de Saint Jacques for presenting the king with twelve vessels of war, "*en pur don et par munificence.*"[3] Again, on the failure of Ribaut's colonizing expedition in 1562, and the massacre of its leader by the Spaniards, a gentleman of Gascony, Dominique de Gourgues, in order that the act might not go unpunished,

[1] Doneaud, ch. i.
[2] Guérin, *Histoire Maritime de France*, t. II., p. 69.
[3] Eugène Sue, *Histoire de la Marine Française* (Paris, 1845), t. I., p. 17.

equipped three vessels and "*exerça sur les Espagnols de sanglantes représailles.*"[1] In the preceding century there were numerous cases of this sort; and it is interesting to note that Jacques Cœur (afterwards so poorly recompensed!), was accustomed to furnish Charles VII. whole fleets at his bidding; and that in 1403 a party of Norman gentlemen partially "conquered" the Canaries.[2]

Nevertheless, from the time of St. Louis the French monarchs had really been struggling to centralize their marine. In 1270 the title of Admiral was borrowed from the Arabs and conferred upon Florent de Varennes; in 1322 Charles IV. created the dignity of Grand Admiral. Meanwhile there had begun the great quarrel with England, which lasted almost without intermission till 1493, and which arose out of piracy or "spoil" claims on both sides. The facts were, substantially, that in 1292 some Norman sailors complained of English piracies to Philippe le Bel, who without investigating the matter authorized them to use reprisals. Accordingly, "on their first rencontre with an English ship, they attacked it, took it, and hung between two dead dogs *(pendirent entre deux chiens morts)* a majority of the crew."[3] It was obvious that, to maintain peace with the hardy English, it would be necessary to subject the piratical Normans and Britons to the curb of a strong central authority, and this authority naturally formed around the person of the Admiral as a nucleus. The judicial functions of the Admiral certainly ante-date 1350, for in that year an Ordonnance was issued giving an appeal to the royal courts from the Admiral's jurisdiction in Normandy.[4] The extent of those functions does not seem to have been definitely determined until Charles V., in December, 1373, issued an Ordonnance providing that the Admiralty should "take

[1] Doneaud, ch. i.   [2] Guérin, t. I.   [3] Guérin, t. I., p. 230.
[4] Pardessus, *Collection des Lois Maritimes* (Paris, 1837), t. IV., p. 224.

jurisdiction, both civil and criminal, *of all acts* committed on the sea and its dependencies" *(connoît de tous faits sur la mer et ses dépendances, tant criminellement que civilement)*.[1] As one of the droits of his office, the Admiral became accustomed to claim as his share one-tenth of all prizes taken.[2] In order that this tenth might be secured, as much as for the protection of neutrals, it was necessary that prizes should be brought in for fair adjudication in an unpillaged state, and it was also necessary to keep account of those who were engaged in the work of making prizes. The *Règlement sur le faict de l'Admirauté* of July, 1517,[3] provided, that if prizes were not brought in, or were brought in pillaged, the offenders should be punished at the discretion of the Admiral *(seront punis à la discretion de nostredit Admiral, etc.)*. Much earlier than that, as early in fact as 1400, privateers were required to obtain the consent *(congé et consentement)* of the Admiral before starting on a cruise.[4] By ordonnances in 1398 and 1498 they were required to give security not to injure any but the enemy.[5] It is to be noted that the distinction between a privateer's commission and a letter of mark and reprisal was just as clear in France as in England. The former was always issued by the Admiral, the latter only by the king personally. Two early

---

[1] Pardessus, *Collection des Lois Maritimes* (Paris, 1837), t. IV., p. 224.

[2] *Ibid.*, p. 295, Ord. of March, 1584. " . . . et de toutes les prises faites . . . nostredict Admiral aura son droict de dixiesme."

[3] Lebeau, *Nouveau Code des Prises, ou, Recueil des édits*, etc. (Paris, an VII.), t. I., p. 5. See, for two cases of punishment occurring in 1696, *ibid.*, pp. 229, 230.

[4] Lebeau, t. I., p. 1. Ordonnance du 7me Dec., 1400. Art. 3 provides: "Se aucun de quelque estat qu'il soit, mettoit sus aucun navire à ses propres despens pour porter guerre à nos ennemis, CE CERA PAR LE CONGÉ ET CONSENTEMENT DE NOSTREDICT ADMIRAL ou son [lieutenant, le quel a ou aura au droict de sondit office la cognoissance, jurisdiction, correction et punition de tous les faits de ladite mer et des dépendances, criminellement et civillement," etc.

[5] Lebeau, t. I., p. 80, note.

attempts of the Parlement de Paris to assume sovereign functions in this particular[1] were effectually deprived of all value as precedents by the Ordonnance of 1485.[2]

The dignity of Admiral at last became attended with so many burdensome feudal privileges, and became moreover so purely honorary in its nature, that Richelieu took the bold step of procuring its abolition, and the substitution for it of the post of "Grand-maître, chef et surintendant" of the marine.[3] The advantages which the navy derived from being placed under the immediate control of the energetic cardinal-duke instead of the feeble and nominal leadership of Henri de Montmorenci, may best be observed in the exploits of D'Harcourt, Pont-Courlay, Jourdis and Brézé, during the Thirty Years' War, in the rise of the naval "arsenals" of Havre, Brest and Brouage, and the increased attention to naval matters, and particularly to the teaching of naval discipline, in the Académie Royale.[4] The national interest in the navy had been excited in 1627, by the defeat of the large English fleet sent to the relief of La Rochelle, and by the consequent reduction of that centre of disturbance. Richelieu's efforts to encourage private adventurers, however, seem to have met with but little success,[5] and his good work for the regular marine was all undone under Mazarin, who prac-

[1] Arrêt du 12me Juillet, 1345, and 14me Fév., 1392.
[2] Lebeau, t. I., p. 104, note.
[3] Édit of Oct., 1626. By an édit of January, 1627, the ancient office of connétable was also abolished, and Louis the Just, perhaps for fear of changing his mind, added the following: "Défendons à toutes personnes généralement quelconques, etc., de quelque dignité, qualité et condition qu'elles soient, de nous demander ou faire demander aucune des dites charges, *sous peine de nôtre indignation*."
[4] Doneaud, ch. i.
[5] "The despotic governments of Paris and Madrid," says Crowe, "vainly strove to imitate the freer Dutch. Capitalists would not trust the lawless extortions of absolute minister and monarch" (*History of France*, Vol. III., p. 468). This is particularly true of the crafty, parsimonious ministry of Mazarin.

tically let the navy perish for want of supplies. But seventy hulks, and little or nothing of the adventurous spirit which had existed among the upper classes in the reign of Francis I. and Henry IV., remained to the French marine when Colbert, on March 7, 1669, procured for himself the position of Ministre Secrétaire d'État.

2

From Colbert to the Peace of Versailles (1783).

If we regard legislation only, the period from Colbert's appointment till the battle of La Hogue, in 1692, would not seem to have been very favorable for the development of privateers. The prodigious centralization which Louis XIV. loved fell heavily upon the liberty-loving freebooters. Everything was regulated for them in advance. The security which they must give (formerly, by the Ordonnances of 1398 and 1498, required only in general terms), was fixed at 15,000 livres by the great Marine Ordonnance of 1681.[1] They were forbidden to ransom their prizes above a certain sum.[2] Baïonne was the only town excepted from the rule that privateers must carry at least six guns.[3] Further, the post of Admiral was revived in favor of the Comte de Toulouse, a natural son of the king, with the provision that a prize court should meet in his house " when he should be of

[1] Titre des prises, Art. 2. Lebeau, t. I., p. 80. Art. 1 provides that a commission shall be necessary, and that the Admiral shall have one-tenth of all prizes and ransoms. Art. 1 of the Ordonnance provides that justice shall be administered in the name of the Admiral in all Admiralty courts. For the full Ordonnance see Pardessus, *Collection des Lois Maritimes*, t. IV., p. 325.

[2] The Ordonnance of Feb. 6, 1697, made this sum 30,000 livres for privateers in America. Formerly it had been 15,000 livres. Lebeau, t, I., p. 233. Privateers were forbidden to ransom *prisoners*, under heavy penalties, by the Ord. of Oct. 9, 1666. Lebeau, t. I., p. 45.

[3] Ord. June 14, 1691. Lebeau, t. I., p. 139. The exception was on account of the little corsaires of Biscay.

an age to participate therein";[1] and not only were private adventurers once more compelled to share their prizes with this carpet sailor, but also to give up a percentage of one denier per livre on what remained to them, to the marine hospital at St. Malo.[2] An additional three deniers per livre was required in the ports of Bretagne and Granville for the ransom of sailors captured in Barbary or the Levant,[3] and at Calais, by custom, one-half of one per cent. went to the poor.[4]

In spite of these burdensome regulations, this was the beginning of the Golden Age of the French corsaires. The vigorous Colbert, by his encouragement of commerce, his protection of naval industries, and his enormous increase of the *matériel* of the royal navy, which grew in his hands from seventy vessels in 1666 to 196 in 1671, 276 in 1683, and nearly 300 at his death,[5] succeeded in raising in the coast towns a mighty wave of enthusiasm. So many private adventurers appeared that corsaires began to travel in squadrons, the idea of uniting them being popularly attributed to Jean Bart.[6] The highest personages in the realm, according to Maurice Loir,[7] did not disdain to make fortunes out of privateers.

Saint-Malo became such a "nest of corsaires" that the English conceived the plan of exploding an infernal machine in that port; the project, however, was a failure, and covered its inventors with ridicule. The profitableness of privateering at this time may be inferred from the fact that on one day alone—Monday, Sept. 25, 1690—Jean Bart took four

---
[1] "Lorsqu'il sera en âge d'y assister." Ord. Oct. 21, 1688. Lebeau, t. I., p. 110.
[2] Arrêt du Conseil, Mai 29, 1690. Lebeau, t. I., p. 135.
[3] Arrêt du Conseil, Fév. 26, 1691. *Ibid.*   [4] *Ibid.*, p. 136.
[5] Doneaud, ch. ii. See generally Beckford's *History of France*, Vol. IV., p. 69
[6] Larousse, *Grand Dict. du XIXme Siècle*, tit. Jean Bart.
[7] *La Marine Française*, Paris, 1893, p. 74.

Hanseatic vessels, which he ransomed then and there for 39,000 livres;[1] and on the 19th and 20th of the same month he had taken four others, the aggregate ransoms of which amounted to 40,500 livres.[2] The war from 1681 to 1688 was remarkable for the outrages committed by French privateers upon Dutch fishermen. These outrages were encouraged by the government, on the very satisfactory ground that the fisheries "afforded almost the subsistence" of the Dutch.[3] Acts of piracy of course became very frequent; and, in 1689, an example was made of the crews of some privateers which had, "as a last exploit, pillaged a neutral ship."[4] "Such scandals," says Loir, "were common; they announced the decadence of our marine."

The French privateers in Europe, however, appear on the whole to have been comparatively temperate and law-abiding sailors, fearing God and the king, and respecting neutrals. But in America there had developed what may be called a school of privateering, in which no fear of any kind was known and no respect entertained. The *flibustiers*, or Bothers of the Coast, had begun to be heard of in the war of the Devolution (1667), in which the services that they rendered to France were so great that their excesses were overlooked. Frequently starting out in fishing boats, which they forcibly exchanged for merchant vessels or small privateers, these men often ended their cruises on a public ship of war; and their ambition increased in proportion to their successes. The prizes which they took were rarely heard of by the admiral. Captured crews were graciously dismissed if their vessels were richly laden; if not, they were mercilessly

---

[1] Eugène Sue, *Hist. de la Marine Française*, t. IV., p. 289.   [2] *Ibid.*

[3] *Mémoire d'Hubert à Colbert sur les Armements en Course à Dunkerque*, Sue, t. III., p. 316. This, says Hubert, is to the Dutch "d'autant plus sensible qu'elle fournit presque la subsistance de leur pays."

[4] Loir, *La Marine Française*, p. 76.

obliged to walk the plank.[1] During the Devolutionary war some *flibustiers* landed in Venezuela and ransomed the town of Maracaibo, which the inhabitants had prudently abandoned at their approach. Pillage, of course, preceded the ransom, the ransom money being paid merely to prevent the unpillaged residue from being set on fire. The spoils of Maracaibo, and of the Yucatan peninsula, which was ravaged about the same time,[2] were piously sent to enrich various West Indian chapels.

At first these depredations were confined to the enemy and to time of war; but after the Peace of Nimègue, in 1678, the *flibustiers* had become so numerous, and were so unfit for any other occupation, that their ravages continued unabated. Twelve hundred of them pillaged Vera Cruz and put it to the enormous ransom of 10,000,000 livres, half of which was paid in slaves. Another band descended on Guyara, in Venezuela, and carried off the governor and garrison. An English vessel, cruising harmlessly around La Tortue, was visited and searched, and on the captain's saying that the sea was free and that he was merely taking the air (*qu'il se promenait, que la mer était libre, et qu'il n'avait sur cela aucun compte à rendre*),[3] his crew were put to the sword and his vessel treated as prize. Grammont, the hero of this exploit, when told before one of his expeditions that Louis XIV. disapproved of them, is said to have replied: "How can Louis XIV. disapprove of a design of which he is igno-

---

[1] "Ils obtenaient la vie," says Guérin, t. III., p. 185, "si les galions qu'ils ramenaient du Nouveau-Monde étaient bien chargés d'or, d'argent, de pierreries ou d'autres richesses; mais si l'espérance du vainqueur était deçue, alors malheur à eux! on les jetait impitoyablement à la mer!"

[2] Larousse, tit. *Flibustiers*. The *flibustiers*, he says, never commenced their repasts without saying their prayers; which would be more edifying if he did not add, "in order that heaven might send them victory and a rich prize (pour que Dieu leur accordât la victoire et une riche capture)."

[3] Guérin, t. III., p. 413.

rant, and which is only a few days old?" Three of Grammont's colleagues, De Graff, Jonqué and Michel Basque, had the effrontery, after hovering around Carthagena and capturing two vessels of war which the governor despatched against them, to send him a letter announcing that they would wait fifteen days for more; which, however, never came.

In 1691 war broke out between England and France, and Bayonne, St. Malo and Dunkirk sent out swarms of corsaires. Duguay-Trouin, then seventeen years old, led his first expedition to Ireland, where he landed, ravaged a "château" and burned two vessels which he could not take home.[1] At the same time Jean Bart and Forbin made a descent on Scotland, and burned four villages and one castle, from which they carried all the valuables,[2] besides destroying several vessels.

In 1692 occurred the naval disaster of La Hogue, the effect of which was to disperse the French fleet collected under Tourville for the invasion of England, so as hopelessly to prevent its reunion. Louis XIV., who for some time had been lending vessels of state to private individuals, was now reduced altogether to this expedient, and the restrictions formerly placed upon the obtaining of public vessels were removed. The Ordonnance of Oct. 5, 1674,[3] providing that only fifth-rate vessels should be devoted to such uses, and then only with the express consent of the king; and that of the 8th Nov., 1685,[4] allowing the individual adventurers in such cases only one-third of the booty, gave way to the Ordonnance of Oct. 6, 1694,[5] providing that after the admiral's tenth and an amount equal to one-fifth of the remain-

---

[1] Guérin, t. IV., p. 10. Guérin adds, with pardonable air of pride, "Voilà quelles étaient les prouesses de Duguay-Trouin, à peine entré dans sa dix-huitième année." [2] *Id.*, p. 11.

[3] Lebeau, t. I., p. 64. [4] *Id.*, p. 109. [5] *Id.*, p. 193.

ing nine-tenths for the king, the adventurers should be entitled to all the residue. The king's share was given up during the war of the Spanish succession (Ord. July 1, 1709).[1]

From the battle of La Hogue till the Peace of Ryswick in 1697, the European privateers were accordingly very active and numerous. Morel of St. Malo took, in a fortnight, twenty-two considerable prizes; and if we may believe the accounts of Frenchmen, Duguay-Trouin with one companion took, in one engagement, two English men-of-war and twelve merchant vessels.[2] Jean Bart created for himself such a reputation that in 1692 the Prince of Orange, sailing from Holland and observing the French corsair pursuing him with an inferior force, is said to have lowered the pennant of his vessel in order that Bart might not know which was his.[3] The great Dunkirkian received his letters of nobility in 1694; in 1696, single-handed, he broke up the enemy's herring fishery, and thus destroyed the means of livelihood of the crews of about 500 boats. In America, the *flibustiers* surpassed all previous records. Ducasse, the governor of St. Domingo, placed himself at their head, and organized two expeditions against Jamaica, ravaging everything, destroying the fortifications and carrying off about 3,000 slaves. In 1697, in conjunction with the royal officer De Pointis, Ducasse and the *flibustiers* took Carthagena in the Indies by assault, and De Pointis having appropriated an unfair share of the booty, they revenged themselves upon the unfortunate town, which, altogether, was made to yield about twenty million livres.[4] The Marquis of Nesmond is said to have made 10,000,000 by one venture against the Dutch.[5] Lemoyne D'Iberville drove the English out of Hudson's Bay;

[1] Lebeau, t. I., p. 339. [2] Guérin, t. IV., p. 29.
[3] Abbé Margon, *Mémoires de Tourville* (Guérin).
[4] Doneaud, ch. iii. [5] *Ibid.*

and all this with the regular navy weaker than it had been at any time since Colbert.

The close of the reign of Louis XIV. is marked by further centralizing legislation, more or less burdensome to private adventurers. An arrêt of 1695 put a stop to the issue of privateer-commissions by the governors of the West India islands[1]—a measure which was most oppressive to the *flibustiers*, with whom the governors had usually been in league. On the other hand, the necessity of a commission was rigorously insisted on; and in 1706 a prize taken by an uncommissioned cruiser was adjudged to the King.[2] A clerk (*écrivain*) of the admiralty was assigned to every privateer, with power to receive the papers of all captured ships and seal up their cargoes to await trial.[3] Further, the percentage for the marine hospital was raised to six deniers per livre[4] instead of one; three deniers per livre were required for the use of sailors wounded on board privateers;[5] and in Dunkirk there was an additional tax for the benefit of widows.[6]

Nevertheless, the activity of the French corsaires continued during the war of the Spanish succession. The *flibustiers*, in spite of the "amnesty" granted them by the crown,[7] never fully revived after the Peace of Ryswick; but the European

[1] Arrêt du Conseil du 14me Mai, 1695. Lebeau, t. I., p. 206.

[2] *The Success*, Arrêt du Conseil du 23me Jan., 1706 (*Id.*, p. 307). Similar decisions had been rendered in 1661 by the Conseil des Prises. Later, in 1761, four English vessels captured by uncommissioned adventurers were adjudged to the Admiral—(*Jugement du Conseil des Prises*, Jan. 31, 1761. Lebeau, I., p. 639). In 1694 the *Charles Pink* was adjudged to the captors, but by the consent of the Admiral. *Id.*, p. 191.

[3] *Ordre de l'Amiral*, Avril 20, 1697. Lebeau, t. I., p. 239.

[4] Édit. de Dec., 1712. *Id.*, p. 399.

[5] Arrêt du Conseil, Mars 31, 1703. *Id.*, p. 273.

[6] Arrêt du Conseil, Juillet 24, 1703. *Id.*, p. 277.

[7] Ordonnance du 1er Juin, 1707. Lebeau, t. I., p. 326.

adventurers were very numerous and active. The death of Jean Bart was almost compensated for by the rise of St. Pol, who became the scourge of the Dutch fishermen. Forbin in the Adriatic distinguished himself by the partial burning of Triest, and by his conduct in regard to the Venetians, whose neutrality he doubted, and the suspected cargoes on whose ships he made a practice of throwing overboard. In 1708 the two captains D'Aire spent three days in pillaging the little Portuguese town of Porto-Santo in the Canaries. Duguay-Trouin, like Jean Bart, was given letters of nobility, and indeed he merited them, having destroyed or taken in his short career no less than sixteen vessels of the line and over three hundred merchantmen. A colossal private expedition of Duguay-Trouin's, in 1711, defeated an entire Portuguese fleet and captured Rio de Janeiro. In the last two years of the war the vigorous Cassard succeeded in temporarily reviving the *flibustiers;* one of the Cape de Verde islands was taken and its capital pillaged; Montserrat and Antigua were reduced, a Dutch colony ransomed, and St. Eustatius and Curaçao compelled to capitulate.[1] This is the close of the most successful period of French privateering; yet so little is the Peace of Utrecht a brilliant victory for France, that Chateaubriand calls this war, of all the wars of Louis XIV., "*the most just in its principle and the most unhappy in its results.*"[2] The treaty with England contained the humiliating provision that France should demolish the fortifications of Dunkirk.

The same treaty also regulated the issue of letters of mark. It provided that "all letters of reprisals, of mark or of countermark, heretofore issued, are revoked; and none shall hereafter be issued except in the sole case of a denial of justice (*si ce n' est seulement en cas de déni de justice*) and then

[1] Doneaud, ch. iii.
[2] Chateaubriand, *Études Historiques*, p. 544.

only on four months' notice to the ambassador or representative of the offending state.¹

Under the vacillating administration of Louis XV., the French marine underwent a steady decline. A bungling colonial policy succeeded the far-reaching designs of Louis the Great. In spite of the Peace of Aix-la-Chapelle in 1748, the English and French went on fighting in India; and the recall of Dupleix, at the critical moment, by the cabinet of Versailles, shows indeed that Louis XV. was guided by men who "sought more for dividends than empires."² Privateers appeared in the war of the Austrian succession, and the two Bacheliers and De Cock, of Dunkirk, acquired some reputation; but as a whole, the corsaires were affected by the spirit of decadence which possessed the royal marine, and enterprise of all kinds languished.

The weakness of France was apparent to her enemies, and, unwillingly enough, she was again compelled to encounter England as an adversary in the Seven Years' War.

The English depredations upon French commerce anterior to the declaration of war led to a curious revival of one of the spectacles of times long past. A merchant of Marseilles, one Georges de Roux, having had eight of his vessels taken by the English, and unable to persuade the cabinet of Versailles to take any decisive action, himself issued a manifesto against England, and sent forth, at his own expense, seventeen vessels to make reprisals.³ When Louis XV. at last determined upon war, he had recourse to the same heroic measures for encouraging privateers that the English had adopted at the opening of the century. The burdensome share of the Admiral, which had been suspended in 1748,⁴

[1] Art. 16.
[2] " . . . qui ne demandaient que des dividendes, et non des royaumes."— Doneaud, ch. iv.
[3] Roux, *Histoire du bailly de Suffren*, referred to by Doneaud, ch. iv.
[4] Déclaration du 5me Mars, 1748, Lebeau, t. I., p. 523.

was again suspended in 1756,[1] and finally and forever abolished in September, 1758.[2] Practically the whole property in the prizes was given to the captors, with the usual result of immediately bringing out a great many little and very active privateers, which made the sea intolerable for neutrals, and indirectly enriched the state, but exercised no influence whatever on the ultimate result of the war. While Thurot was landing in Ireland and ransoming Carrickfergus, the British were driving the French out of India and Canada; and the exploits of Dumont de Lisle, Morel and De Cock did not rescue Louis XV. from the necessity of concluding in 1763 a peace which all Frenchmen agree in terming "deplorable."i

The death, in 1764, of Mme. de Pompadour, to whom a great deal of the decadence of the navy was due, was followed by some tardy attempts on the part of the Choiseul ministry to revive the marine. The continuation of these attempts by Louis XVI. had placed the royal navy once more on an excellent footing, when the American Revolution began; and the burning desire of the whole nation to wipe out the disgrace of the Peace of Paris led inevitably to the American alliance of 1778. This war, culminating in the triumphant Peace of Versailles, is perhaps the most respectable period in the history of French privateering. Louis XVI., having observed the successes of the privateers of the United States, immediately determined to encourage them in France as they had never been encouraged before. Heavy "gratifications" or bounties based on the number of guns and prisoners taken were promised by the *Déclaration Concernant la Course*, June 24, 1778;[3] the whole property

[1] May 15. Lebeau, t. I., p. 541.   [2] *Id.*, p. 512.

[3] *Id.*, t. II., p. 23. "SAVOIR—100 livres pour chaque canon du calibre de 4 et au-dessus jusqu' à 12 livres; 150 livres pour chaque canon de 12 livres et au-dessus; et 30 livres pour chaque prisonnier fait; sur les navires charg:s en marchandises," etc. The figures were 150, 225, and 40 livres respectively on the enemy's privateers captured; and 200, 300, and 50 on his men-of-war.

was given to the captors, and there were provisions for the dispensing of arms from the royal arsenals, in order to reduce the cost of equipping private expeditions. For the first time corsaires were to be allowed to carry the white flag "fleurdelysé."[1] By the treaty of amity and commerce between France and the United States, the privateers of either nation were permitted to carry their prizes into the ports of the other,[2] so that French privateers cruising off Canada were not obliged to carry prizes to the West Indies. Notwithstanding the swarm of corsaires which instantly appeared under these favorable conditions, the wise and temperate regulations of Louis XVI. kept them fairly within bounds. For the first time, they were forbidden to interfere with the coast fisheries (*la pêche côtière*).[3] They were commanded to observe the "utmost circumspection" with regard to the vessels of Russia, Sweden, Denmark and Holland,[4] who were being gently led by the crafty Vergennes into the Armed Neutrality which, as has been seen in another chapter, proved so embarrassing to the enemy. In 1782 the Swedish ship *Argos*, unlawfully captured by a British cruiser and recaptured by the French privateer *La Joséphine*, was restored *with damages, interest and costs*,[5] and in the same year the admiralty at Dunkirk was instructed to punish the *Éclipse* for her pillage of a Danish vessel.[6] As a further illustration of the moderation of Louis XVI.'s privateering, we may refer to the strenuous orders given in 1779 that corsaires

[1] Guérin, t. V., p. 70.

[2] Art. XVII. *Treaties and Conventions between the United States and other Powers* (Washington, 1889), p. 301.

[3] *Lettre du roi à l'amiral.* June 5, 1779, Lebeau, t. II., p. 102: ". . . pourvu toutefois qu'ils ne soient armés . . . et qu'ils ne soient pas convaincus d'avoir donné quelques signaux qui annonceroient une intelligence suspecte avec les bâtimens de guerre ennemis."

[4] *Lettre du roi à l'amiral,* Aug. 7, 1880, Lebeau, t. II., p. 256.

[5] *Arrêt du Conseil,* Apr. 8, 1782, Lebeau, t. II., p. 398.   [6] *Id.,* p. 453.

should respect Captain Cook, and treat him as neutral so long as he remained engaged in discovery only.[1] The period of war from 1778 to 1783 was for the corsaires a period of effectiveness, and effectiveness with honor. It closed with the Peace of Versailles, and nothing like it was ever seen again in France.

3

The Era of Revolution

The formidable navy developed by Louis XVI. was, of course, completely disintegrated in the early stages of the revolution. The banishment of its chiefs, the abolition of the office of Grand Admiral, the transfer of the administrative power formerly possessed by naval officers to civil officers of the ports,[2] the merciless bigotry towards everything aristocratic which brought the able and honorable D'Estaing to the guillotine, the substitution everywhere of incompetence for experience, reduced the French marine from the position of a navy to that of a mere collection of armed vessels with crews. When the execution of Louis XVI. (Jan. 21, 1793) converted the wavering neutrality of England into open hostility, and the French ambassador was told to leave England within eight days, there was a great cry for privateers; and on Jan. 31 the National Convention enacted as follows:[3]

"Art. 1. French citizens may fit out privateers *(pourront armer en course)*.

"Art. 2. The Minister of Marine, to accelerate private armaments if there shall be any, shall deliver letters of mark, or permissions in blank to arm for war and cruise against the enemies of the Republic."

[1] *Arrêt du Conseil*, Apr. 8, 1782, Lebeau, t. I., p. 83.
[2] See Guérin's comments on the decrees of Sept. 21, 1791 : t. V., p. 295.
[3] Lebeau, t. III., p. 44.

The fourth article of the same "law" provided that *only one-sixth of the total number of registered sailors should be allowed to engage, at a time, in privateering.* Had it not been for this provision, there would have been none left for the regular navy. As it was, the Convention was compelled to lay an embargo on all privateers until the vessels of the line had made up their armaments.[1]

On February 1 war was formally declared against England; on the 2nd the Convention adopted the first of what may be called its starvation measures, by offering a premium to corsaires bringing in enemy vessels laden with grain.[2] It had become apparent that the Allies were endeavoring to starve France into submission, and heroic measures had to be taken to obtain food, which was already beginning to be regarded as "contraband" by English cruisers, and pre-empted as such by the doubtful admiralty courts. On the 9th of May the Convention issued a very famous decree,[3] reciting the conduct of the English with regard to provisions, and the capture, by an English privateer, of a Danish ship carrying provisions from Dunkirk to Bordeaux; and ordering the seizure and pre-emption of all provisions bound for ports in the possession of Great Britain. This decree marks the beginning of a long series of disputes between France and the United States. Mr. Morris, the American minister at Paris, instantly objected to the decree of the 9th of May as a violation of Art. 23 of the treaty of amity and commerce of 1778. On May 23 the Convention, therefore, excepted American vessels from the operation of the decree; and M. Le Brun, Minister for Foreign Affairs, communicated the new decree to Mr. Morris, with the remark that it was a "confirmation of the

[1] *Loi du 22me Juin*, 1793, Lebeau, t. III., p. 80.
[2] *Loi du 2me Fev.*, 1793, Lebeau, t. III., p. 51.
[3] *Am. St. P., For. Rel.*, I., p. 748.

principles from which the French people will never depart with regard to their good friends and allies, the United States of America."¹ On May 28, however, the decree of the 23rd was repealed; the repeal being due to the influence of the captors of a very rich American ship (the *Laurens*) who wished it condemned.² On July 1 the convention again excepted American vessels—"a new proof," according to M. Le Brun, "of the fraternal sentiments of the French people for their allies."³ The fraternal sentiments lasted till July 27, when the excepting decree was again repealed, and the decree of the 9th of May left in force.

By this time the regular navy of France had become the laughing stock of Europe. Under the laws made for it by the civil officers appointed by the Convention, and particularly by the notorious Jean-Bon-St.-André, a French vessel was forbidden to surrender, unless sinking, to vessels of the enemy, *whatever their number*, under pain of treason. The ferocious *Représentant* of the Convention also forbade the taking of prisoners, and commanded that merchant vessels captured be sunk "*jusqu' aux équipages.*"⁴ Yet, as has almost invariably happened in French history, the more demoralized the regular marine became, the more bold and successful became the private adventurers. From Feb. 1, 1793, to the close of the year 1795, the French corsaires took 2,099 prizes; and the loss of the French merchant marine was only about 319.⁵ Robert Surcouf had begun his work; Moultson in 1795 captured a large part of the Jamaica fleet; and Richéry's expedition to Labrador broke up the fisheries and sank 80 vessels engaged in that trade. The discomfort in England was great. The funds fell, the

¹ Report of Timothy Pickering, Secretary of State, communicated to Congress, Feb. 28, 1798, *Am. St. P., For. Rel.*, I., 744 *et seq.*
² *Ibid.*   ³ *Ibid.*
⁴ Guérin, t. VI., p. 20.   ⁵ *Id.*, p. 110.

Bank of England suspended specie payments, the British flag was swept out of the Mediterranean; yet the ancient enemy of France could not be brought to terms, but kept up the struggle long after her allies had abandoned it.

In the mean time the complications between France and the United States had become alarming. The first minister of the revolutionary government received by the United States, Genêt, had at the outset entertained the hope of dragging the United States into the war. In accordance with this idea, he had, without seeking permission, fitted out in American ports a number of privateers, to which he distributed commissions or letters of mark which he had brought already signed in blank from France. The proclamation of neutrality issued by Washington on April 22, 1793, was not believed by Genêt to be regarded with favor by the Republican party; and upon its enforcement by the administration he appealed to the people, found the Federalists too strong for him, and, on the demand of Washington, was recalled. Meanwhile, the privateers fitted out under his commissions had made several prizes (some of them within the territorial waters of the United States), which the French consuls in our ports had assumed authority to condemn; and the resulting claims of Great Britain, which the administration recognized as just, were charged on our growing account with France.

The conduct of the French cruisers had at the same time been becoming more and more insupportable. Mr. Fulwar Skipwith, in his report of October, 1794, to Mr. Monroe, in Paris,[1] complained that many American vessels were rendered unseaworthy by being stripped "of their officers and crews, which are generally replaced by boys and inexperienced hands, in order to be conducted to ports." The *Alexander* laden with flour *on account of the French government*, was

[1] *Am. St. P., For. Rel.*, I., 750.

captured August 5, 1794, and carried to Rochefort, "being stripped of all her crew except the cabin boy," and so rendered unseaworthy.[1] The ship *Mary*, London to Boston, was captured by a French cruiser, and *her passengers plundered of their hats and watches;* the cabin was entirely ransacked; "the passengers, though late at night, and the sea running extremely high, were hurried into a small boat and sent at some distance on board the sloop of war." Among the passengers were several women.[2] The executive directory, by the decree of July 2, 1796, commanded French cruisers to treat neutrals as the latter "allowed" themselves to be treated by the English; which amounted to a license to deal with neutrals at discretion. The agents of the executive directory in the Leeward Islands, of whom the infamous Victor Hugues was one, decreed, on November 27, 1796, the capture of all American vessels bound to or from British ports, thus anticipating the Berlin decree by ten years. The stuff of which this Hugues was made may be gathered from his conduct in the case of the *Patty*, captured September 5, 1796. According to the affidavit of the master, Josiah Hempstead,[3] he was immediately taken before Hugues, "whose first words addressed to me were, 'I have confiscated your vessel and cargo, you damned rascal,' doubling his fist and running it close to my face." Later, September 8, Hempstead asked when his vessel and cargo were to be tried, and "he answered that they had been already tried and I might go about my business." An old and obsolete marine ordinance[4] requiring neutral vessels to carry a *rôle d'équipage*, or certified list of passengers and crew, was revived by a decree of March 2, 1797 (17me Ventôse an V.),[5] and the

[1] *Am. St. P., For. Rel.*, I., 750.   [2] *Id.*, p. 751.
[3] *Id.*, p. 759. See also generally, *John Adams' Works*, VIII., 551.
[4] *Règlement du 23me Juillet*, 1704.
[5] *Am. St. P., For. Rel.*, III., 284.

want of such a list was frequently "deemed sufficient to warrant the condemnation of American property, although the proofs of the property were indubitable."[1] Many American vessels, like the *Patty*, were condemned in the West Indies without even allowing a defence or looking at the papers.[2] As for the privateers, all discipline seemed lost. The brig *Resolution* was captured in 1796 by a privateer, and the skipper stripped of everything, "even his clothes."[3] The *Delight* was condemned in St. Domingo before her captor arrived, for having no sea-letter,[4] the sea-letter having been forcibly detained by the privateer herself.[5] Another French cruiser forcibly placed twenty prisoners upon the *Mermaid*;[6] another plundered at sea the schooner *Hank*, Jamaica to Philadelphia, and then dismissed her;[7] another plundered the brig *Sally*, and "also flogged the captain;"[8] another fell upon the *Nancy*, and stripped the crew of their clothes, even the shirts from their backs, drove them below, beat them with cutlasses, and placed them on a diet of bread and water;[9] two others fired thirty shots into the brig *Almy*, "although she was, and had been some time previous, lying to for them;"[10] another pillaged the mate's chest of the schooner *Two Friends*;[11] another broke open and plundered the cargo of the *Success* on the high seas;[12] another stole provisions from the ship *Pattern*. The *Commerce* was raked fore and aft by the French privateer *La Trompeuse*, "not

---

[1] *Report of Sec'y of State*, 1797, *Am. St. P., For. Rel.*, II., p. 29. [2] *Ibid.*
[3] Sam'l and Ed. Cutts to Sec. of State, Apr. 3, 1797.
[4] *Registry of the Sec'y of the Provisional Tribunal of Prizes established in St. Domingo*, 13me Ventôse, an V.
[5] Affidavit of Mark and John Hatch, 10th May, 1797.
[6] *Am. St. P., For. Rel.*, II., p. 59.   [7] *Id.*, p. 60.   [8] *Ibid.*
[9] Affidavit of J. Smith, May 13, 1797.
[10] Affidavit of J. Mitchell Cutter, Oct. 20, 1796.
[11] Affidavits of Van Renssalaer and O'Quin.   [12] *Am. St. P., For. Rel.*, II., 60.

being the length of a ship away, after having hove to and distinctly answered twice."[1] The sloop *Kitty* was summoned to lie to with the formula, "Damn your eyes, hoist your boat out." Said the Secretary of State in his report of June 21, 1797: "The persons also of our citizens have been beaten, insulted and cruelly imprisoned; and in the forms used towards prisoners of war, *they have been exchanged with the British for Frenchmen.*"[2] The prize courts were debauched utterly; the sloop *Fox* was condemned without the shadow of a cause, "the owners of the privateers having given the commissioners 100 half joes to pronounce that sentence."[3]

The following, among other remarkable cases, are mentioned in the Philadelphia *Gazette :*

(1) A French privateer boarded Captain Pierce, of Philadelphia, and besides stealing about $300, beat his supercargo with a sword so that he died. On complaint to the French authorities, the privateer was imprisoned three days.[4]

(2) The *Zephyr* was plundered of all her provisions by the French privateer *Hirondale;* her captain, who had begged to be allowed to remain on board the privateer, was ordered on shore, and finally thrown overboard.[5]

(3) The *Two Sisters*, Norfolk to Leogane, was boarded by a French privateer, and two sailors compelled, at the point of the cutlass, to sign a declaration, written in French, that the destination of the vessel was Jamaica; on the strength of which declaration she was sent in and sold, and the purchaser put in possession; after which the papers were sent to Cape François for trial.[6]

Perhaps the most outrageous case of all, however, was that of William Martin, who was thumbscrewed for three hours in the cabin of a French armed brig, sailing under English

[1] Affidavit of Andrew Frothingham and William Watson, Jan. 1, 1797.
[2] *Am. St. P., For. Rel.,* II., p. 29.   [3] *Id.,* p. 60.
[4] *Phil. Gaz.,* 28th Nov., 1796.   [5] *Id.,* 5th Apr., 1797.   [6] *Id.,* 6th Apr., 1797.

colors, because he would not acknowledge that his cargo, belonging to a Baltimore firm, was English property.[1]

The depredations of the *Fortitude*, a privateer which took and burned an English merchant vessel, the *Oracabissa*, within the territorial waters of the United States,[2] at last forced the issue between the United States and France. On July 10, 1798, the President, in pursuance of acts of Congress passed May 28, June 20 and July 9, instructed the commanders of armed vessels of the United States "to subdue, seize and take any armed French vessel or vessels sailing under authority or pretence of authority from the French republic, which shall be found within the jurisdictional limits of the United States or elsewhere upon the high seas."[3] Privateers were also sent out by the United States; several naval engagements occurred, and several French vessels were taken and condemned as good prize. Hostilities were terminated by the convention of 1800,[4] which provided for a "firm and inviolable" peace, the restoration of public vessels captured, the repression of piracies and the requirement of security before issuing privateer commissions, to the amount of $7,000, or 36,820 f., for a vessel carrying fewer than 150 men, and double that sum for a vessel carrying more than 150 men. The convention also contained a most-favored-nation clause, and re-established the rule Free Ships, Free Goods. About the same time the Second Armed Neutrality checked the French corsaires in Europe, and

[1] Letter from Rufus King, Apr. 19, 1797, enclosing the protest of William Martin, dated Apr. 3, 1797, *Am. St. P., For. Rel.*, II., p. 64.

[2] Message of John Adams, Feb. 5, 1798, transmitting letter of Charles Pinckney, Governor of South Carolina, of 22d Oct., 1797. John Adams' *Works*, IX., 155.

[3] Report of Committee of the House of Representatives, Apr. 22, 1802, *Am. St. P., For. Rel.*, II., 459.

[4] Concluded Sept. 30, 1800; ratifications exchanged at Paris, July 31, 1801; proclaimed Dec. 21, 1801.

caused the First Consul to do his utmost to regulate those in America, in order to obtain the good-will of the northern powers, already prejudiced against England.

The Peace of Amiens was violently broken by the British embargo of May 15, 1803, which Napoleon answered by ordering the arrest of all the English in France (May 22). The convention, already (April 30) concluded, for the cession of Louisiana to the United States, was quickly ratified, and the First Consul, no longer obliged to defend this burdensome possession, found himself free to develop at leisure his scheme of Continental Blockade. The French privateers in America, again allowed to run wild, resumed their career of piracy. In consequence of their depredations, American merchant vessels began to travel armed, and to resist visit, which furnished a pretext for the French to treat them, in turn, as pirates. "Nothing saved our lives," write three of the crew of such a vessel, "when they boarded us, but their thinking we were English, and asked us how dare we engage under American colors."[1] A "black general" is said to have committed suicide rather than fall into the hands of the French.[2]

Meanwhile the blows to neutral commerce in Europe were beginning to fall in quick succession. The exclusion of British vessels from certain German and nominally neutral ports was followed by the British declaration of blockade of May, 1806, from the river Elbe to the port of Brest. On November 21 of the same year, Napoleon, having defeated the Prussians at Jena and triumphantly occupied Berlin, felt himself strong enough to retaliate upon Great Britain for this absurd and illegal blockade, and accordingly issued the Berlin decree, declaring the whole British Isles blockaded, ordering the arrest of all Englishmen and the

[1] P. Sisson, etc., to G. Barnewall, Esq., July 26, 1804, *Am. State Papers, For. Rel.*, II., 608.
[2] *Ibid.*

confiscation of their property, half the proceeds of which was
to be applied to the indemnification of Continental merchants
who had been damaged by unlawful seizures on the part of
British cruisers; and forbidding the entry into French ports
of any vessel direct from England or her colonies. Notwithstanding the broad language of the decree, the French minister of marine succeeded, on December 24, 1806, in satisfying
the American minister that nothing new was intended.
Indeed, the Berlin decree was not known to have been
enforced against American commerce until October 10,
1807, when the *Horizon* was condemned.[1] The British Order
in Council of January 7, 1807, cannot, therefore, be justified
as a counter-retaliation for the Berlin decree,[2] though perhaps the more vexatious Orders of November 11 may
justly be referred to that ground. On December 17 the
Emperor issued the Milan decree, continuing the paper
blockade of the British Isles and forbidding neutrals to "sub-
mit" to the Orders in Council of November 11th, under pain
of becoming "denationalized" and liable to capture as British; which provisions were said to be merely a *juste recip-
rocité* for the conduct of Great Britain. The embargo ordered
by the Congress of the United States in December, 1807,
furnished Napoleon with a shallow pretext for another sweeping decree, aimed directly at the United States. On April
17, 1808, orders were given "to seize all American vessels
now in the ports of France, or which may come into them
hereafter,"[3] on the ostensible ground that since the embargo
no American vessel could legally leave home, and, therefore,
any found in the ports of France were presumptively navi-
gating on British account; whereas, it was matter of common knowledge that a great many American vessels had

---

[1] Report of Committee of House of Rep., Nov. 22, 1808, *Am. State Papers,
For. Rel.*, III., 259. [2] *Ibid.*

[3] Bayonne Decree, *Br. & For. State Papers*, VIII., 484.

deliberately remained abroad in order to avoid the embargo, without ceasing in any respect to be neutral. The embargo in the United States having become worse than war, it was dissolved in March, 1809, and war determined upon; but, unwilling to inaugurate a "three-cornered" struggle, the American government pursued the policy of "auction sale," offering, practically, if either side should repeal its decrees, to go to war with the other. An ambiguous announcement, on August 5, 1810, that the Berlin and Milan decrees should cease to have any effect after the first of the succeeding November,[1] was hailed with joy by the American public, or rather by the Republican part of that public, and treated as an actual repeal; and the matter was believed to be settled by the decree of April 28, 1811.[2] Subsequent investigation disclosed the discomforting fact that the Republican party had been tricked by Napoleon, who never had any real intention of repealing his decrees at all, and who, by a *secret* decree, since known as that of Trianon, had kept alive the mischief which his official decree of April, 1811, had purported to abolish. However, it has been seen that the repeal of the British Orders in Council, which was delayed till June 23, 1812, was not influenced in the slightest degree by the supposed repeal of the decrees of Berlin and Milan, and, therefore, with our national chagrin for having been so easily trapped by Napoleon, need be blended no regret for having unjustly attacked Great Britain.

As to the fall of Napoleon, it is necessary to remark only upon the well-known fact, that his Continental System, his own creature, was his ruin. It was the attempt to extend that system which led to the disastrous breach with Russia; and from Moscow to Elba was at most but a question of time.

[1] *Cf.* Guizot, *Histoire de la France*, 1789–1848, t. II., p. 168.
[2] *Report of Sec'y of State*, July 12, 1813; *Am. State Papers, For. Rel.*, III., p. 609.

Yet the exultation of Great Britain was tempered somewhat by the results of the American war. The treaties of 1814 and 1815 were not so much triumphs for Great Britain as they were triumphs for neutrals. If, as Doneaud says, they "gave the earth to Russia," they emphatically did *not* give England the sea.[1]

[1] " En résumé, ces traités donnaient la mer à l'Angleterre; la terre, à la Russie." Doneaud, ch. vi.

CHAPTER III

PRIVATEERING IN THE UNITED STATES

I

During the Revolution

FROM 1756 to 1763 the privateers fitted out in the North American colonies of Great Britain, and particularly in the ports of Massachusetts and Rhode Island, had inflicted enormous injuries upon the commerce of France. The New England sailors had taken to privateering naturally, and as naturally had laid it aside upon the conclusion of the Peace of Paris. It might have been expected, therefore, that upon the outbreak of hostilities with the motherland in 1775, the colonists would be prompt to effect a second transition, and resume the marauding rôle in which they had already become distinguished; but for various reasons this did not happen immediately.

The conflict which began in April, 1775, was a domestic dissension between Great Britain and her colonies. The American nation, though struggling for birth as it had been struggling for the previous decade, was not yet born; and properly speaking, therefore, the hostilities at Lexington were not the beginning of a *war*. The situation of the colonies was peculiar. Congress vacillated. One day full of fire and threats, the next, conciliating and hopeful that the ministry were at last coming to their senses, it was impossible to force it into any definite course; and the resulting handicap upon the colonists was severe. It was on account of this state of things that no privateers were commissioned by the central government in 1775.

The first naval victory of the colonists, nevertheless, was the result of private enterprise. On May 5, 1775, some people of New Bedford and Dartmouth fitted out a vessel with which they entered a harbor of Martha's Vineyard and cut out another American vessel, of which the *Falcon*, a British cruiser, had made prize.[1] On June 11 the king's cutter *Margaretta* convoyed two sloops to the harbor of Machias, there to be freighted with lumber for the use of the army in Boston. The sloops were promptly seized by the townspeople, and a certain Captain O'Brien, with forty companions, was despatched in one of them against the cutter, which, after some resistance, struck her colors.[2] These trifling successes aroused the most intense enthusiasm, particularly in New England; and the desirability of extending hostilities to the sea in a systematic manner began to be felt immediately. On June 12, Rhode Island commissioned two vessels,[3] and the other maritime colonies, as if they had merely been waiting for the signal, followed suit. In November, Massachusetts authorized private-armed vessels to cruise, and established a court for condemning their prizes.[4] In the meantime the inertia of Congress was beginning to give way before the sturdy attacks of the delegates from Rhode Island, who, on Oct. 3, had laid before the body of their peers their instructions of the preceding August, to use their whole influence for equipping a continental fleet.[5] Washington was in favor of the project; for it was a source of great annoyance to him to see British transports and store

[1] Winsor, *Narrative and Critical History of America* (Cambridge, 1888), VI., p. 564.
[2] Bancroft's *Hist. of the U. S.*, IV., 184. [3] Winsor, VI., 565 n.
[4] *Gent. Mag.*, Jan., 1776; referred to by Winsor, VI., p. 591.
[5] Bancroft, IV., 263.

ships passing him *unarmed*, and to be obliged to refuse his men "leave to put a few guns on board a vessel to cruise for them"[1] until he had communicated with the Congress. The successes of the few impromptu cruisers which he did send out in this way, in intercepting stores, made him the more anxious that their number should be multiplied; indeed, Mr. Cooper considers that, if it had not been for the supplies thus brought in, "the Revolution must have been checked in the outset."[2] John Adams also lent his support to the Rhode Island delegates; and, on the 13th of October, Congress passed a resolution directing the equipment of two national cruisers, the first of which was to carry "ten carriage guns, with a proportionable number of swivels."[3] Thirteen frigates were ordered in December,[4] and while they were being constructed merchant vessels were commissioned by Congress as vessels of war, and merchant captains as naval officers. The *personnel* of a navy was as difficult to find as the *matériel;* for nearly all the colonists whose sons had a taste for the sea had sent them into the British navy, from which scarcely any resigned.[5] Under these circumstances Congress at length adopted the inevitable policy of authorizing private individuals to cruise. On March 23, 1776, a resolution was passed "that the inhabitants of these colonies be permitted to fit out armed vessels to cruise on the enemies of these United Colonies."[6] The preamble simply recited that an "unjust war" was being urged against

---

[1] Adams to Langdon, Jan. 24, 1813; John Adams' *Works*, X., p. 27.

[2] *History of the Navy of the U. S.*, ch. xiii.

[3] Emmons, *Statistical History of the Navy of the U. S.*, p. 204; Cooper, ch. iv.; *Journals of Congress*, I., 219. On Oct. 30 it was resolved that the second vessel carry 14 guns. *Journals of Congress*, I., 227.

[4] *Journals of Congress*, I., 292.

[5] Cooper, *History of the Navy of the U. S.*, ch. iv.

[6] *Journals of Congress*, Vol. I., p. 296.

the colonies; that their petitions were unheard; that an act of parliament [1] had declared their trading vessels good prize; and that it was "justifiable to make reprisals" upon their "enemies." On April 3 it was resolved [2] that "blank commissions for private ships of war, and Letters of Marque and Reprisal, signed by the President," be sent to the different States; the security to be given by applicants for such commissions or letters was fixed at $5,000 for vessels under 100 tons, and $10,000 for larger vessels, in either case payable to the President of Congress in trust for the use of the United Colonies; and all applications were to contain a description of the vessel and crew, etc., "and the quantity of provisions and war-like stores," and were to be forwarded to the Secretary of Congress and by him registered. Elaborate instructions for the guidance of the privateers thus commissioned were issued on the same day. Articles 1 and 2 of these instructions authorize them to "attack, subdue and take" British vessels (with certain exceptions in favor of immigrants), or vessels carrying contraband to the British, wherever found on the high seas, or between high and low water-mark. The succeeding articles provide for bringing the prizes in "to some convenient port or ports in the United Colonies;" for "severe punishment" of any one killing or maining a prisoner; and for written accounts of captures to be sent to Congress "by all convenient opportunities." Article 8 contains the singular provision that one-third at least of their whole company shall be "landsmen." Article 9 forbids them to "ransome any prisoners or captains;" and the tenth and last article reserves the right to issue other instructions from time to time, if necessary.

[1] The 16 Geo. 3, c. 5. See Frothingham's *Rise of the Republic of the U. S.*, p. 486.

[2] Force, *American Archives*, Fourth Series, vol. V., p. 1443 *et seq.*

The privateers which rapidly took the sea under these instructions were unlike any which the world had ever seen before. It would be idle, of course, to pretend that they were all inspired by patriotic motives only; but it is certain that the patriotism of most of them was of a purer character than that of their English and French predecessors. For the first time in its history the privateer-system assumed approximately the shape of a marine militia or volunteer navy. Nothing so well illustrates this fact as the generous readiness of our early privateers to place themselves under general naval control for the purpose of helping along any maritime adventure. Continental ships, the vessels of the state navies, and private individuals frequently joined in dangerous and often pecuniarily unprofitable ventures, for the general good of the cause; and the spectacle of three privateers uniting with regular war-vessels in an attack upon the transports sent to Howe in June, 1776,[1] was a unique one. Frequently, also, perhaps too frequently, they actually went out of their way to attack vessels of the British navy, and sixteen of His Majesty's cruisers figure prominently in the list of their prizes.[2] It was this admirable, yet misdirected zeal that Adams so much deplored when, writing to Calkoen in 1780[3] he said that *had it not been for their imprudence*, the American frigates and privateers would " by this time, well-nigh have ruined the British commerce, navy and army."

Towards the close of 1776 a new and magnificent prospect began to open for private vessels of war. On October 1,

[1] Winsor, VI., p. 568. See also Cooper, ch. xii. In January, 1778, an American privateer assailed in the night the British fort of New Providence in the Bahamas, capturing the fort and a sixteen-gun man-of-war. Jameson's *Dict. of U. S. History*, tit. *Privateers*.

[2] Maclay, *Hist. of the Navy*, Part I., ch. viii.

[3] Adams, *Works*, Vol. VII., p. 266, at 312.

Silas Deane, who was then in Paris, wrote to Congress[1] to send over a number of blank commissions, or preferably "a general power for that purpose;" "for," said he, "*it is certainly a very practicable and safe plan to arm a ship here, as if for the coast of Africa or the West Indies, wait until some ship of value is sailing from England or Portugal, slip out at once and carry them on to America.*" The nations of Europe being at peace, Deane was able to be "acquainted with the time of every vessel's sailing, either from England or Portugal," so that the prospect was a very alluring one indeed. In another letter[2] he counsels the sending of a couple of frigates to the Banks to break up the fisheries, which had already had one "wretched season" on account of our privateers; and he suggests that Congress may buy ships on credit from French merchants at 5 per cent. In December, Congress authorized the fitting out in France of "any number of vessels not exceeding six, at the expense of the United States, to war upon British property.[3] The nation was five months old, and Congress was losing its timidity. The sympathy of France was notorious. The jubilant privateers knew, with the rest of the world, that France was in the war in spirit, and might at any moment enter it in form. Great Britain knew it best of all, but put off the evil hour as long as possible. At no other time could Vergennes, in answer to Lord Stormont's complaints that French officers were embarking for America by scores, have risked his witty reply that the French nation "had a turn for adventure."[4] The Treaty of Utrecht provided that it should not be lawful "for any foreign privateers to fit their ships in the ports of one or the other of the aforesaid

[1] Deane to Committee of Secret Corresp., Sparks' *Dip. Cor.*, I., 43.
[2] Same, Nov. 27, 1776, Sparks' *Dip. Cor.*, I., 66.
[3] *Secret Journals of Congress*, II. (For. Aff.),35, 36.
[4] Bancroft, V., 126.

Partys,"[1] yet Americans armed ships daily in the harbors of France. In violation of the same treaty they carried their prizes in and sold them; Vergennes extricating himself on the plea that he could not eject foreign vessels in distress. Distress, of course, became a chronic condition of the American privateers in European waters; and if, in consequence, any controversies arose between the French court and our commissioners, they were designed solely for publication in the London *Gazette*.

Meanwhile the misery inflicted by our privateers on the ubiquitous British commerce was steadily increasing. They came forth from New England in an endless stream, Rhode Island, which was particularly active,[2] sending forth in 1776 no less than fifty-seven.[3] New England, in fact, had begun to live on privateering; in Salem it was the principal business of the town.[4] Even outside of New England, men like Washington[5] and Morris[6] engaged in it. Early in 1778, Mr. Woodbridge reported to the House of Lords that 733 vessels had been captured since May, 1776—a loss to the nation of £1,800,633 18s;[7] but even this enormous total gives but a faint idea of the damage done by our cruisers. The West India trade was almost ruined. With one-fourth of the ships taken, with insurance at 23 per cent., with rum and sugar falling 11 per cent. on account of the colonial demand being shut off, and with the inevitable delays, it is estimated[8] that the losses to that trade amounted to 66 per cent. Nor was the European trade safe. Thanks to the

[1] Quoted by Winsor, VI., 570.
[2] Lossing, *Field-Book of the Revolution* (N. Y., 1859), I., 641.
[3] Sheffield, *Privateersmen of Newport*, Appendix XI.
[4] *Salem Gazette*, quoted in Niles, *Am. Rev.* (Baltimore, 1822), p. 378.
[5] See MS. letter of Washington, Nov. 14, 1777, to Custis, quoted in Lossing's *War of 1812*, p. 998.   [6] Lossing, *Field-Book of the Rev.*, II., 638.
[7] *Records of Parliament*, Vol. XIX., pp. 707–711; referred to by Maclay, *Hist. of the Navy*, Pt. I., ch. v.   [8] Niles, *Am. Rev.*, p. 432.

hospitality of France and the indecision of Spain, our privateers swarmed in European waters, and even the channels and the Irish Sea were not free from them. So great was the unrest that *linen ships from Dublin to Newry sailed under convoy;*[1] and ten per cent. insurance was sometimes paid from Dover to Calais.[2] The result was to drive trade almost entirely into neutral bottoms; and the Thames "presented the unusual and melancholy spectacle of numbers of foreign ships, particularly French, taking in cargoes of English commodities for various parts of Europe."[3] Apropos of the capture in the Channel of a British brig of two hundred tons by a privateer of twenty, Mr. Carmichael gaily wrote:[4] "I had been told by a man high in office in England that resistance was a chimera in us, since their armed vessels would swarm so much in our rivers as even to interrupt the ferry-boats. *His assertions are verified vice versa; our ferry-boats ruin their commerce.*"

The comparative purity of motive of the "ferry-boats," as a body, did not save Congress from the complications with neutrals, which are the common curse of too much privateering. The neutrality of Spain was quite serious at first; and an American captain who put into Bilboa with his prizes in October, 1776, was arrested and tried for piracy,[5] escaping conviction only with considerable difficulty. In 1777, our commissioners at Paris began to be "much troubled with complaints of our armed vessels taking the ships and merchandise of neutral nations,"[6] Holland complaining of the

[1] *Annual Register*, 1778, p. 36, quoted by Whart., *Dip. Cor.*, II., 168 n.
[2] Winsor, VI., 574.
[3] *Annual Register*, 1778, p. 36, quoted by Whart., *Dip. Cor.*, II., 168 n.
[4] Carmichael to Dumas, June 13, 1777, Sparks, *Dip. Cor.*, IX., 323.
[5] Deane to Committee of Secret Corresp., Nov. 27, 1776, Sparks, *Dip. Cor.*, I., p. 54.
[6] Franklin, Deane and Lee to the Com. of For. Aff., Nov. 30, 1777, Sparks, *Dip. Cor.*, I., p. 340.

capture of the *Chester* of Rotterdam, Spain of the capture of the *Fortune* laden with Spanish goods, and even friendly France indignant over an attack upon her royal vessel, the *Emperor of Germany*, though willing to pass over with a merely formal protest the arrogance of the Portsmouth privateer in seizing an English merchantman in the very mouth of the Garonne.[1] The "irregularities," or more plainly the piracies, of one Captain Conyngham, who persisted in making Dunkirk the base of his operations, and who was shut out of Spain for his impolitic capture of a Swedish ship with Spanish property, from London to Teneriffe, "cost the public more than 100,000 livres,"[2] and produced a considerable anti-American feeling in Madrid. The zeal of our privateers, most of whom seemed to have been born with a prodigious talent for the making of mischief, led them to burn all the prizes that they could not safely send in; and as there frequently happened to be neutral property on board, they soon came to be liked as little as their brethren of England. It was, however, so obviously the policy of Congress to obtain the good-will of neutral nations, and its efforts in this direction were so marked, that these cases were regarded generally as the excesses of individuals, and led to no serious breach with the United States.

The inevitable Franco-American alliance was concluded in February and went into effect July 17, 1778. Article XVII[3] of the Treaty of Amity and Commerce, which went hand in hand with the Treaty of Alliance, gave the fullest liberty to privateers and ships of war of either party to make use of the ports of the other. Under these favorable conditions privateering flourished more and more. The

[1] Lee to Committee of For. Aff., Nov. 27, 1777, Whart., *Dip. Cor.*, II., p. 429; and see note to p. 840.
[2] Same, Nov. 15, 1778, Whart., *Dip. Cor.*, II., p. 840.
[3] *Treaties and Conventions of the U. S.*, p. 301.

seventy odd British vessels engaged in blockading our coasts in 1776 and 1777 were compelled to unite in the summer of 1778 in order to meet the fleet despatched from France under D'Estaing; and with nearly all our ports free it was "impossible to conceive the havoc" made by our privateers.[1] The number of prisoners taken was so great that in 1779 Great Britain was at last obliged to consent to a cartel for their exchange. From 1780 till the end of the war privateering was not quite as profitable as during the two preceding years. D'Estaing had unfortunately removed to the West Indies, Sir Henry Clinton had taken Charleston, De Grasse was delayed, and in Europe the Armed Neutrality, though directed primarily against England, chilled the air for all private adventurers. "Nevertheless," says Mr. Cooper, "it is a proof of the efficacy of this class of cruisers to the last, that small privateers constantly sailed out of the English ports *with a view to make money by recapturing their own vessels;* the trade of America at that time offering but few inducements to such undertakings."[2]

To an American, perhaps the most remarkable thing about our privateers is their patriotism. To any one else, that which would appear most remarkable is their success. Our privateersmen started out with the intention of hastening the approach of peace; and there can be no doubt that their influence in that direction was great. The reasons for this influence, which, as has been seen, it is by no means usual for privateers to exercise, are to be found in the peculiar situation of England during the last years of the war. With France, Spain and Holland carrying on a vigorous war, and the Baltic powers united in a sort of morose readiness to join them, the reduction of the colonies by any one brilliant *coup* was impossible. To the ministry, therefore, it was a

[1] Gerry to Adams, May 5, 1780; *Adams' Works*, VII., 189.
[2] *Hist. of the Navy*, ch. xii.

question of recognizing our independence or else temporizing. And here is precisely where the effect of the privateers was felt; for with that mighty force striking unceasingly at its one vital part, its trade, the English nation simply could not afford to temporize. It was less spirited, but more profitable withal, to conclude the Peace of Versailles.

2

During the War of 1812

The poverty of the three Federalist administrations and the political principles of the three Republican administrations which succeeded them, prevented the development of any substantial Federal navy. When Madison sent Congress his war message on June 1, 1812, the available naval force consisted of seven frigates and about a dozen smaller vessels, many of which were unfit for sea. The British navy at the time consisted of 1060 sail,[1] and it was believed by the opponents of the war in New England that with this tremendous force our adversary might institute a blockade of our coasts three or four vessels deep and yet have some to spare. With a wisdom born of experience, Congress decided to lose no time in calling for private vessels of war. The declaration of war itself[2] conferred authority upon the President "to issue to private armed vessels of the United States commissions or letters of marque and general reprisal, in such form as he shall think proper, and under the seal of the United States." Eight days later an act was passed[3] regulating the issue of commissions in detail. It contained the usual provisions for a written description of the vessel to be filed with the Secretary of State, for security of five or ten

[1] Coggeshall, *Hist. of Am. Privateers*, ch. ii., referring to *Steel's List of the Royal Navy*, 1811-2.
[2] June 18, 1812; 12th Congress, First Sess., chap. cii.; 2 *Stat. at L.*, 755.
[3] June 26, 1812, 2 *Stat. at L.*, 759.

thousand dollars according to the number of the crew (150 *men* and not 100 *tons*, as in the Revolution, being made the point of distinction), for the transfer of the whole property in the prizes to the captors, subject to their written agreement; for the bringing in of these prizes and their adjudication in the district courts of the United States; for the delivery of prisoners to a United States marshal or other district officer; for a bounty of $20 for each man alive on board hostile ships of equal or superior force at the beginning of the engagement leading to their capture; for journals of cruises to be kept under penalties, and shown on demand to the public vessels of the United States; and for obedience to any instructions issued by the President. Subsequently the President authorized Mr. Monroe, Secretary of State, to issue the customary instructions. As the war was undertaken by the United States in defence of neutral rights, the second paragraph was made particularly explicit upon this point:[1]

"2. You are to pay the strictest regard to the rights of neutral powers and the usages of civilized nations. * * * You are particularly to avoid even the appearance of using force or seduction with a view to deprive such [neutral] vessels of their crews or of their passengers. * * *"

Circumstances were particularly favorable for privateering. For nineteen years American shipping had had to run the gauntlet of vexatious French decrees and British orders, under such conditions that visit meant capture; and the safety of every vessel had depended not upon her papers but upon her sails. Necessity had produced during this period a great number of fast-sailing clippers which were ready at any time to be converted into privateers; and under the act of June 26 the conversion instantly began.

[1] See Guernsey, *New York City during the War of 1812*, vol. II., App. n. 4; and Whart., *Dig.*, § 385.

Notwithstanding the unpopularity of the war in New England,[1] and the abhorrence of privateering which had developed in some parts of it,[2] the parts which were not thus affected responded to the call for private armed vessels with a rich though sulky generosity which astonished the peace party in England. Traders "delirious with disaffection" equipped privateers,[3] and Salem was not far behind Baltimore in the number which she sent out. One month after the declaration of war a little volunteer navy of sixty-five vessels was at sea, and the prizes were beginning to arrive almost daily.[4] "Any craft that could keep the sea in fine weather"[5] set out to watch for British vessels unsuspiciously approaching the coast, and scores of pilot-boats armed with one or perhaps two nine- or twelve-pound guns, reaped rich harvests during the first few weeks of the war. Our shipping, of course, did not suffer proportionately. In the first place there was less of it—less even than usual, for a great deal of it had been converted during the preceding decade into nothing more substantial than French Spoliation Claims; and besides, the provident embargo of April 4, 1812,[6] just before the declaration of war, had kept a great deal of what still remained to us at home. Those who objected to the war as suicidal on the part of the United States saw only one side of the picture. They did not see, and hence derived no comfort from, the exhaustion under which our adversary was laboring. Her trade taken by surprise,

[1] See *Hildreth's Hist. of the U. S.*, III., p. 372.

[2] All the apothecaries of New Bedford refused to fill the medicine chest of a ship's doctor, who said his ship was a privateer which had come into New Bedford to refit. For its encouragement of privateers Baltimore was branded by the *Mercury* of the same town as a " sink of corruption" and the " Sodom of our country." Ingersoll, *Second War with Great Britain*, Second Series, vol. I., p. 31.

[3] *Ibid.*, p. 26.   [4] Coggeshall, ch. ii.

[5] Henry Adams, *Hist. of the U. S.*, VII., p. 314.

[6] 2 *U. S. Stats. at L.*, p. 700.

her prestige lost by the surrender of the *Guerrière*, gold at 30 per cent. premium, wheat nearly five dollars a bushel, Wellington retreating in Spain and Napoleon to all appearances about to crush the Czar,[1] the most sanguine minds in England were profoundly uneasy. In 1813 the outlook became a little brighter. Napoleon was evidently beaten, and the danger of invasion was past; the American coast, moreover, was closely blockaded, and the pilot-boat privateers were abandoned as useless; but the distressed state of the country continued, and the mercantile and shipping classes, whose arrogance had produced the Orders in Council and brought on the war, raised loud cries for peace. The one force that produced these cries for peace was the American privateers. Not the American army, for its successes were interrupted and indecisive; not the regular navy, for its destruction of British prestige maddened while it did not exhaust the enemy; but the five hundred odd clippers which did not fight, but which sailed as only Yankee clippers can sail, and took, and burned, and destroyed—these were the real peace-makers.

Through the negligence of the admiralty, the British cruisers in the Windward Islands had been out so long that their copper was almost off, and in that region, in consequence, our privateers became "so daring as even to cut vessels out of harbors * * * and to land and carry off cattle from plantations"[2]—a source of great mortification to the London *Times*. As British vessels were now rarely met except armed or in convoy, the privateers of 1813 were larger and stronger than those of 1812; but their sailing qualities are universally conceded to have been the finest in the world. In a light breeze, or for sailing into the wind, they had no

[1] Henry Adams, *Hist. of the U.S.*, VII., p. 5.
[2] Letter to the *Times*, Dec. 30, 1812; quoted in Henry Adams' *Hist. of the U. S.*, VII., p. 12.

rivals; and it was not unusual for them to sail from a blockaded port fearlessly in broad day-light, if they were able to get the blockading squadron to leeward. How much we depended on these little vessels to bring about a disposition for peace in England before Napoleon was crushed and we were left alone against her, was becoming apparent to Congress, and the year 1813 contains quite a deal of "encouraging" legislation of all kinds. A bounty of $25.00 for each prisoner taken by privateers was offered on Aug. 2,[1] and increased to $100.00 in March of the next year.[2] The history of the privateer pension fund begins with the act of June 26, 1812, which directed 2 per cent. net of every prize to be paid over to the collector of the port for the use of widows, etc.; the distribution was regulated by the acts of Feb. 13 and Aug. 2, 1813.[3] The system of destroying prizes was now in high favor in the Department of the Navy. All the regular war-vessels were practically instructed to destroy their prizes, being assured by the Secretary of the Navy that, unless very valuable, and near a friendly port, "it will be imprudent, and worse than useless, to attempt to send them in."[4] About one-half of the vessels sent in were re-captured, on account of the strictness of the blockade, and it was felt to be a great pity that privateers, as well as regular war vessels, could not be induced to destroy all that they captured. "Encourage them," wrote Jefferson—the same Jefferson, by the way, who had helped negotiate the treaty of 1785 with Prussia—"to burn their prizes, and let the public pay for them. They will cheat us

[1] 3 *U. S. Stats. at L.*, 81.   [2] 3 *Stats. at L.*, 105.

[3] 2 *Stats. at L.*, 799; and 3 *Stats. at L.*, 86. See also the Act of Mar. 4, 1814, 3 *Stats. at L.*, 103.

[4] Instructions to commanders of the *Constitution*, the *Siren*, the *Rattlesnake* and *Enterprise*, the *Peacock*, the *Wasp*, etc. *Am. State Papers, Nav. Aff.*, I., pp. 375, 376.

enormously. No matter; they will make the merchants of England feel, and squeal, and cry out for peace."[1] This was the true principle. By an act of March 3, 1813,[2] Congress offered to pay, to any persons who should "burn, sink or destroy" any British *armed* vessel of war, one-half the value of such vessel. Jefferson's idea was, substantially, the extension of this act to all captured vessels whatsoever, and such an extension would, it is conceived, have been excellent economy. One-half the value of the prize at the moment of capture was fair, because the chance of its reaching port safely was only about one-half; and this system would have prevented the weakening of privateers by the constant withdrawal of prize crews, a weakening which always rendered them inefficient and frequently led to their capture. A bounty of this sort, coupled with positive instructions to privateers to burn their prizes, would have been the true policy of our government; and not, as Mr. Henry Adams suggests, the total abolition of privateering and the equipment of fifty sloops-of-war like the Argus.[3] Fifty vessels, however well managed, cannot do the destructive work of five hundred; and moreover, under such an arrangement as the one suggested, privateers would be quite as efficient as sloops-of-war, besides costing the public less.[4] The burning of vessels without trial usually produces ill-feeling and diplomatic difficulties, but it is not illogical to claim it as a belligerent right, as long as capture of enemies' property at sea is recognized. The vessel burned is either wholly hostile, in which case certainly no one has any right to complain; or hostile with neutral property on board, in which case

[1] Jefferson to Monroe, Jan. 1, 1815, *Writings of Jefferson*, VI., 407 at 410.
[2] 2 *U. S. Stats. at L.*, 815.   [3] *Hist of the U. S.*, VII., p. 335.

[4] Mr. Henry Adams says (VII., p. 335) that the privateers cost the government more than than the sloops would have cost, on account of the pensions and bounties. He forgets that the sloops too would have had to have pensions and bounties, besides being equipped and sailed at the government's expense.

the neutral takes the risk of the destruction of the vessel by the other belligerent; or wholly neutral (the fourth case of neutral vessel and enemy property being eliminated by the rule Free Ships Free Goods). If wholly neutral, of course, it would unquestionably be an outrage to destroy it, unless, indeed, by reason of some irregularity in its papers, its neutrality should not have been fairly apparent.

As it was, the privateers burnt a good many vessels without instructions. The *Governor Thompkins* and the *Surprise* each destroyed 14; the *Fox* and the famous *True-Blooded Yankee* 7 each; the *Grand Turk* 6, and nearly every privateer which took prizes had one or two burnings to its score.[1]

Privateering in 1814 was very popular in New York. The total number of cruisers sent out from New York City during the war was 120, and they brought in 275 prizes, and sunk and destroyed many more.[2] One New York privateer brought in booty to the amount of $300,000, after having narrowly escaped from seventeen successive British pursuers.[3] So much was cruising against the British coming to be regarded as a sort of legitimate commercial business, that in October, 1814, the legislature of New York passed an "Act to encourage privateering Associations"[4] which contained the most elaborate provisions for the formation of *stock corporations* to carry on privateering. By this time the merchants of England were heartily sick of the war and complained bitterly, sometimes to the Admiralty, sometimes to the Prince Regent himself. The British Isles, for the second time, were really in a state of blockade; not a block-

---
[1] See the list of captures in Emmons' *Statistical History of the Navy of the U. S.*
[2] Guernsey, *New York City during the War of 1812*, Vol. II., Appendix, note 4.
[3] Lamb and Harrison, *Hist. of the City of New York*, p. 654.
[4] *Laws of N. Y.*, 38th Sess., chap. xii.

ade of the Napoleonic kind, but of a substantial, dangerous sort which caused insurers to demand the enormous premium of 13 guineas on £100 across the Irish Channel, in spite of the three frigates and fourteen sloops which were constantly on duty protecting it.[1] At Halifax, insurance was practically refused; sometimes 35½ per cent. was paid. The *Morning Chronicle* complained that "that the whole coast of Ireland from Wexford round by Cape Clear to Carrickfergus" was blockaded by "a few petty fly-by-nights."[2] In spite of the heavy tax paid by merchants as "convoy duty," the Admiralty was unable to afford them protection; the *Governor Thompkins* cruised leisurely through the channel, burning fourteen vessels in her passage, and the *True-Blooded Yankee* destroyed twenty-seven in thirty-seven days. The United States sloop-of-war *Argus* made her headquarters in St. George's Channel and averaged a prize a day; everything taken was burned, under the instructions before quoted. Undoubtedly Great Britain was the principal sufferer by the war; moreover the situation had become somewhat ludicrous, for the Orders in Council had long been repealed, and after the recent naval events it was hardly necessary for Great Britain to bind herself on paper not to maltreat American vessels in the future. And so, for the second time, a peace was hastened, if its very terms were not influenced, by American privateers.

It is common to regard the Treaty of Ghent as a technical if not a substantial humiliation for the United States, because the British government was not forced into a formal relinquishment of its maritime pretensions. Indeed, the casual reader of the treaty could not but gather the impression that the high contracting parties had been engaged in a very

[1] Coggeshall, ch. ix.
[2] *Morning Chronicle*, Aug. 31, 1814; quoted in McMaster's *Hist. of the People of the U. S.*, IV., p. 115.

bitter boundary dispute, being otherwise on excellent terms. As a matter of fact, of course, the United States never undertook to secure from Great Britain a paper acknowledgment that she had been wrong. The war was resolved upon simply because it was better to have war on both sides than war on the British side and peace on our own.[1]

During the war of 1812, the United States lost some five hundred vessels.[2] According to Emmons, who furnishes perhaps the most reliable statistics of our privateers, the latter alone took from the British 317 ships, 538 brigs, 325 schooners and 161 sloops—1,341 prizes in all.[3] The total number of prizes at sea was probably even greater than this,[4] and Emmons does not count those made on the Lakes. The prizes were, of course, very irregularly distributed. Out of 517 privateers in Emmons' list, only 209 are recorded as ever having taken a prize; on the other hand, 13 are recorded as having taken over 20 prizes each. One of these, the *Yankee*, a brig from Bristol, realized three millions from her captures; they consisted of *nine ships, twenty-five brigs, five schooners and one sloop.*

Thus we emerged from a naval war which we had entered into without a navy and prosecuted against the strongest naval power in the world. If Mr. Gallatin went too far when he called privateering "our only mode of warfare against European nations at sea,"[5] at any rate we must agree with President Pierce, that a proposition to abolish privateering, while

---

[1] Madison's *Message*, June 1, 1812. [2] Coggeshall, p. 395.
[3] *Statistical History of the U. S. Navy.*
[4] Schouler places the number at 1,750 (*Hist. of the U. S.*, II., 455 n.), and Ingersoll at 2,425 (*War of 1812*, p. 117). Coggeshall also says it exceeded 2,000 (p. 395). Probably, however, Ingersoll's and Coggeshall's figures are swelled by captures of American vessels sailing under British licenses, of which a great many were taken and condemned.
[5] Speech of Feb. 10, 1797, Adams' *Gallatin*, 170; Whart., *Dig.*, § 385.

the right of capture of private property at sea remains at all, is a proposition to which "this government could never listen."[1]

[1] Pierce, *Second Annual Message*, 1854, Whart., *Dig.*, § 385.

PART III

THE ABOLITION OF PRIVATEERING

CHAPTER I

THE DECLARATION OF PARIS

THE excesses of the Napoleonic wars had aroused in the habitually neutral states an unconquerable aversion to privateers, which was strikingly evidenced at the opening of the Crimean war. The petty states of Germany, with one accord, shut their ports to all private-armed vessels and their prizes.[1] At the same time, the peculiar and almost unnatural Anglo-French alliance was fraught with happy consequences for neutrals. The British government, in deference to the wishes of its ally, abandoned during the war its ancient objections to the rule that free ships make free goods; and both powers announced their intention not to issue "letters of marque" at all.[2] The sacrifice thus offered up at the shrine of Neutrality was not, it is true, a very great one; for the geographical position of Russia rendered her so susceptible to blockades that the trade in Russian bottoms, never very large, was practically annihilated altogether by a single strong fleet at the entrance to the Baltic; and privateers, if any had been commissioned, would have had to live on neutrals or starve. But the forbearance, on the part of England at least, was so unusual, that when the plenipoten-

[1] *Cf.* the Procl. of the Senate of Hamburg, Apr. 26, 1854 (distress excepted); Procl. of the Senate of Lübeck, Apr. 24, 1854 (distress excepted); Ordinance of the Senate of Bremen, Apr. 28, 1854; Law of Hanover, May 5, 1854; Ord. of Grand Duke of Mecklenburg-Schwerin, Apr. 26, 1854; and, similarly, the Declaration of the Emperor of Hayti, Nov. 18, 1854. *British and For. St. Papers*, Vol. 45, pp. 1269–1277.

[2] *British and For. St. Papers*, Vol. 46, p. 36.

tiaries assembled at Paris to agree on the terms of peace, the smaller states were filled with hopes that something exceedingly liberal, and for the general good of Europe, was about to be accomplished.

The proceedings of the Congress were characterized by more fraternity and good humor than is usual in the discussion of questions relating to the Ottoman Empire. The neutralization of the Black Sea, the regulations about the Danube, and the admission of Turkey into the "European Concert," so increased the spirit of union among the plenipotentiaries that by the time the Treaty of Peace was ready, they were prepared to entertain any liberal idea that their president, Count Walewski, had to propose. The gratifying results of the war, the maritime part of which had been conducted entirely upon French principles, led the latter to propose the permanent incorporation of those principles into International Law. During the séance of April 8, 1856, Walewski, referring to the work of the Congress of Westphalia in establishing freedom of conscience, and that of the Congress of Vienna in abolishing the slave trade and opening the rivers of Europe, remarked that it would be "worthy of the Congress of Paris to end certain disputes of too long standing (*mettre fin à de trop longues dissidences*) by laying the foundations of a uniform maritime law, in time of war."[1] He then suggested the four principles which were afterwards incorporated in the Declaration, the first being the "abolition of privateering."

Lord Clarendon for England announced the readiness of his government to surrender their ancient rights and unite in a declaration that free ships make free goods, *on condition that privateering should be abolished*.

Orloff, for Russia, and Buol, for Austria, promised to ob-

[1] *Brit. and For. St. Papers*, Vol. 46, p. 120; Gourdon, *Hist. du Congrès de Paris*, p. 113.

tain instructions from their governments; and the senior plenipotentiary from Prussia, the Baron Manteuffel, promised the consent of his in advance. At the next conference, April 14, all the plenipotentiaries declared themselves authorized to unite in the following

DECLARATION

* * *

" The Plenipotentiaries,
" Considering,
" That maritime law in time of war has been for a long time the subject of unfortunate controversies,

* * *

" That it is advantageous, in consequence, to establish a uniform doctrine on a point so important,

* * *

have issued the following solemn declaration:
" 1st. Privateering is and remains abolished;
" 2nd. The neutral flag protects the enemy's goods, except contraband of war;
" 3rd. Neutral goods, except contraband of war, are not subject to seizure under the enemy's flag;
" 4th. Blockades, to be binding, must be effective; *i. e.*, maintained by a force sufficient to render approach to the enemy's coast really dangerous.

" The governments of the undersigned plenipotentiaries engage themselves to bring this declaration to the attention of those States which have not been invited to participate in the Congress of Paris, and to invite them to accede to it.

" Convinced that the maxims which they have proclaimed cannot but be received with gratitude by the whole world, the undersigned plenipotentiaries have no doubt that the efforts of their Governments to make their adoption general will be crowned with full success.

"The present declaration is not and shall not be binding except among the Powers which have signed or may accede to it."

On the 16th of April the signatures of the plenipotentaries were formally affixed, and the seven governments of France, Great Britain, Russia, Prussia, Austria, Sardinia and the Porte stood committed to the Declaration. On the proposition of Walewski, "and recognizing that it is to the common interest to maintain the indivisibility of the four principles mentioned in the declaration signed to-day, MM. the plenipotentiaries agree that the Powers which have signed or may accede to it shall not enter for the future, into any arrangement concerning the law of neutrals in time of war, which does not rest on all four of the principles of the said declaration."[1] The Russian plenipotentiaries suggested that this agreement ought not to interfere with any previous conventions; which suggestion was fully approved by the others.

To the casual reader the Declaration, in its completed form, is apt to seem a *monumentum aere perennius* to the wisdom, as well as the philanthropy, of its authors. It cannot be denied, however, that closer examination discloses much that calls for criticism. The professed object of the plenipotentiaries was to establish a "uniform doctrine" on an "important point" which had long been the subject of "unfortunate controversies." Of the four principles enunciated, only one, the principle that free ships make free goods, came within this description. The third and fourth principles had been perfectly settled before, and the *contrary* of the first, that is, that all nations have a right to fit out privateers, had never been questioned; so that these three principles must have been introduced into the declaration for some other purpose than to settle "unfortunate contro-

[1] Protocol 24, *Br. and For. St. Papers*, Vol. 46, p. 137.

versies." Then the "indivisibility" of the four principles is, to say the least, unnatural; and if the plenipotentiaries considered its admission necessary for accession to the Declaration, it was at any rate questionable policy to bind themselves not to "enter, for the future, into any arrangement concerning the law of neutrals in time of war, which does not rest on all four of the principles of the said Declaration." It will readily be seen that this agreement prevents any signatory power from engaging separately with a non-signatory one for the observance of principles (3) and (4), although the latter were simply declaratory of existing International Law; or of principle (2), although the two powers might consistently have practised it, and might have included it in all their former treaties. It was, indeed, rather a defect in the declaration to include principles (3) and (4) at all, especially when there was, as there is yet, a crying need for the definition of contraband, which the Declaration left untouched. The reason for coupling principles (1) and (2) was not a logical, but a diplomatic one. Great Britain, as the strongest naval power, had the greatest interest in abolishing privateering, and without its abolition would never have consented that free ships should make free goods. Of course, if the principles were to be severable, other powers would be enabled to avail themselves of her concession without paying her price; which would indeed be unfair. But that does not excuse the prohibition —suggested by Count Walewski himself—to enter into separate agreements; which strongly savors of discourtesy toward non-signatory powers. Still further, it would have been, it is submitted, in much better taste to word the first article more like a treaty and less like a statute. "*La course est et demeure abolie*" was a very broad statement; it is not too much to say that, in 1856 at any rate, it was a false statement; since it assumed that a principle absolutely new and untried was thereby, with the support of only seven powers, definitely incorporated into International Law. It must be remembered that the first article was the only one which contained an innovation; for (3) and (4) were already admitted by all, and (2) by all except two powers (Great Britain and Spain); yet it is precisely this first article which is worded in the most sweeping and uncompromising way. It was, indeed, this first article which was the *chef d'œuvre* of the Paris Congress.

It is impossible to suppose that the seven great powers who signed the Declaration of 1856 were moved by philanthropy merely. The philanthropic motive was perhaps strongest in France, which has, indeed, always led the way toward a liberal maritime policy, and whose political philosophy was dominated by men who had already come to look with disfavor upon the capture of private property at sea in any way at all. But even France had other motives for her conduct. Her navy was the second in the world, and constantly increasing; and the Declaration, therefore, gave her a tremendous advantage in a maritime war with any of her neighbors except England. Moreover the French privateer, when he existed, was of a more uncontrollable and piratical type than the privateer of England or America; and several decades of spoliation claims had suggested to the French nation that perhaps it was better to save the money which they would have to pay for his depredations, and use it toward carrying on the war. As for the other powers, Russia, Prussia, Austria and Sardinia were no privateering states, and had more to fear from them as neutrals than to gain from them as belligerents; moreover, they received the great concession, Free Ships Free Goods; and Turkey was too young a member of the "Concert" to thwart, by any undue display of individuality, the wishes of all its guardians.

The attitude of England, after the Declaration was signed,

was somewhat peculiar. It is to be remembered that the authority of the British plenipotentiaries was only that of the ministry, who had not, in spite of the great importance of the principles involved, considered it necessary to gain the approbation of the House of Commons, much less that of the House of Lords, before taking the final step. Before very long there began to be an unpleasant feeling that England had been trapped, as the publication of the statistics of the Russian war showed how much more unfavorable to England than had at first been thought was the rule Free Ships Free Goods. One opposition journal declared "Clarendon and his colleagues," for agreeing to the second article, "guilty of a deliberate act of treason against the state, for which they should have been impeached,"[1] and Mr. Lindsay said openly in the House of Commons that "he did not wish to throw aside a solemn declaration, but he said *the people of this country would not abide by it, and would appeal to the House for its abrogation;*"[2] "and it yet remains to be seen," he said later in a letter to Lord John Russell, "whether the chief states of the Christian world would, by force of arms, interpose * * *."[3] The prevailing opinion, however, was that of Lord John Russell, that the Declaration was a *fait accompli*, and that, without regard to the possibility of coercion, a breach of faith could not mend matters.

With its virtues and its faults, the Declaration was submitted for approbation to all the principal states of the world, even to some non-maritime states. Nearly all returned a favorable answer within a few months. Hanover and the Two Sicilies were the first to accede, both notifying the Cabinet of Paris of their intention on May 31; then followed, in order, the Papal States (June 2), Electorai Hesse (June

[1] *London Morning Herald*, Aug. 21, 1856.
[2] Quoted by Aegidi & Klauhold, *Frei Schiff unter Feindes Flagge*, p. 34.
[3] *Ibid.*, p. 45.

4), Tuscany (June 5), Belgium (June 6), the Netherlands (June 7), Oldenburg and Saxe-Altenburg (June 9), Sweden and Norway (June 10), Bremen and the Grand Duchy of Hesse (June 11), Saxony (June 16), Nassau (June 18), Lübeck and Greece (June $\frac{8}{20}$), Saxe-Weimar and Saxe-Coburg-Gotha (June 22), Denmark and Würtemberg (June 25), Bavaria (July 4), the German Confederation (July 10), Mecklenburg-Schwerin (July 22), Portugal (July 28), Baden (July 30), Chili (August 13), Parma (August 20), Mecklenburg-Strelitz (August 25), Guatemala (August 30), Hayti (September 17), Argentine Confederation (October 1), Ecuador (December 6), Peru (November 23, 1857), Brunswick (December 7, 1857), Brazil (March 18, 1858), and Switzerland (July 28, 1858).[1] The notifications of accession are rather interesting documents. Many of them state no reason; a great many descant upon the advantages of the Declaration from the point of view of philanthropy;[2] still others, such as those of Chili, Denmark, the Two Sicilies, the Netherlands, and Portugal, call attention, with much pride, to the fact that the principles just adopted have always been proclaimed by their governments; Baden, Bavaria and Würtemberg are thankful that there are to be no more conflicts about privateers; Guatemala frankly calls the Declaration a *guarantee for weak nations;* the Duke of Tuscany goes so far as to say that he will regard the principles as *making part of his International Law*—though it is doubtful whether by this expression any intention is signified to enforce them against non-acceding powers. The word "his"

[1] *British and For. St. Papers*, Vol. 48, pp. 134-162.

[2] Denmark says its "justice is so evident" (p. 143); Greece considers it (p. 147) a "véritable conquête de la justice et de la science du droit sur les maximes différemment conçues;" it is *rigorous* justice according to Guatemala (p. 148); Hanover calls it "un des plus beaux monuments de la civilisation moderne" (p. 149).

(*son*) would seem to save the remark from the appearance of a threat which it would otherwise possess.

Of all the powers invited to accede to the Declaration, only Spain, Mexico, and the United States returned any answer but an unqualified affirmative. With long coast lines and weak navies, none of these powers could afford unconditionally to abandon privateering; and Spain was not remarkably anxious to establish the rule Free Ships Free Goods, having usually contended for the contrary in her palmiest days. The Spanish nation, moreover, seems to have entertained grave doubts as to the disinterestedness of the greater maritime states in proposing the change.[1] The position of the United States was a difficult one. Always the advocates of a liberal maritime law, it was impossible for us to rest in such bad company as that of Spain and Mexico; on the other hand President Pierce had firmly declared his intention not to agree to the abolition of privateering while capture of private property at sea was allowed at all.[2] On the 28th of July, 1856, Mr. Marcy, Secretary of State, wrote his famous letter to the Comte de Sartiges.[3] After ably criticising the Declaration, pointing out the unfairness of its operation as between powers with weak navies and those with strong ones, and referring to the growing tendency of modern times to separate the government from the individual, of which the Declaration itself was an example, Mr. Marcy abruptly asks why not go the whole way? Why not exempt private property at sea entirely, and thus render the laws of war at sea consistent with the laws of war on land?

"The President, therefore," says Mr. Marcy, "proposes to add to the first proposition in the 'declaration' of the Congress of Paris, the following words: 'And that (*sic*) the

[1] *Cf.* the *Crónica*, Oct. 6, 1856.
[2] Message of Dec. 4, 1854.
[3] *Senate Exec. Doc.* No. 104, 34th Cong., 1st Sess.

private property of the subjects or citizens of a belligerent on the high seas shall be exempted from seizure by public armed vessels of the other belligerent, except it be contraband.'" And he concludes with the hope that the amendment will be accepted, or that the United States will be allowed to join in principles (2), (3), and (4) while holding aloof from principle (1); and with a casual suggestion that it would be as well, in furthering the great purpose of confining the hardships of war entirely to the belligerents, to abolish the law of contraband.

This letter of Mr. Marcy's, at one stroke, took the United States out of the unpleasant position of appearing to obstruct progress, and enabled it, instead of being left an unwilling straggler, to pose as the leader of the van. The logic of the position, from an international point of view, was irresistible. It was difficult for the supporters of the Declaration as it stood to give any legal reason for abolishing privateering, while they recognized the general liability of private property at sea to capture. The arguments against privateering were open to the criticism that they were arguments from the abuse of a thing against its use, and that what privateering really needed was not abolition, but regulation. On the other hand, the world had been drifting toward the principle of the amendment for years. A numerical majority of the nations of the earth was certainly in favor of it. Sooner or later, if the future of International Law was to be judged by its past, it would have to come: why should it not come from the Paris Congress?

The Declaration of Paris was unquestionably an advance —Mr. Marcy's proposition was an advance still greater —and yet it is a matter of grave doubt whether even the latter presented the true solution of the difficulty for the United States. From the international point of view, the Marcy proposition was most commendable; from the point of view of American diplomacy, it is doubtful whether it was wise. Pending the replies of foreign nations, the letter was vigorously discussed by the entire American press. Some papers went so far as to declare the proposed declaration unconstitutional. They maintained that no power was given to the President and Senate to declare away a belligerent right that existed at the formation of the Constitution; that it was even doubtful whether the right could be abolished by constitutional amendment, since, they said, it might well be one of the rights which the Declaration of Independence had referred to as inalienable![1] It was soon seen, however, that this objection was untenable, nearly all our treaties having surrendered some right that "existed at the formation of the Constitution," in exchange for similar concessions on the part of other nations. A more valid objection was that the amendment *as worded* annihilated the Declaration, making articles (1), (2) and (3), or articles (2) and (3) at any rate, unnecessary and tautological, so that it would be scarcely proper to adopt it as an "amendment" in the form presented.[2] Even this, however, was an objection only to the form of Marcy's idea, and not to the idea itself. The genuine and serious objection, from an American point of view, was that Marcy's idea of exemption extended only *to the high seas*, and thus left untouched the system of commercial blockade.[3] The consequences would

[1] *Cf. The National Intelligencer*, Apr. 15, 1857; *London Morning Herald*, Sept. 4, 1856.

[2] *London Globe*, Dec. 22, 1856.

[3] *London Spectator*, Aug. 30; *London Morning Herald*, Sept. 4; *Washington Union*, April 28, 1857; *N. Y. Journal of Commerce*, Dec. 5 (amendment not safe unless blockades [meaning probably commercial blockades] are abolished); *London Times*, July 16, 1857 (would have given England maximum efficiency of navy and minimum risk to commerce). The *Manchester Examiner and Times*, however, Nov. 26, 1856, believed that Marcy's principle, pushed to its legitimate conclusions, would have entailed the abolition of all blockades.

be disastrous in case of war with Great Britain or France, for although they could not capture our property on the high seas, they could, with their immense navies, keep a great deal of it in our ports, while we, not powerful enough at sea to blockade their coasts, would have no means of retaliation. The amendment *as worded* by Mr. Marcy, therefore, presented in one respect a false issue, and would have been almost as unequal in its operation as the Declaration itself.

The English Press was almost evenly divided,[1] but most of the continental papers approved the amendment as offered.[2] Marcy pushed the proposition vigorously, as indeed he did all things. At the same time, it appears that he did his utmost to prevent the smaller states which had not yet acceded to the original Declaration, from doing so. "It does appear to me," wrote Marcy to Dallas, Aug. 4, 1856,[3] "that the proceedings of the Congress at Paris were resorted

---

[1] See for the amendment—
London Morning Chronicle, Aug. 23 and Sept. 2, 1856; *Telegraph,* Aug. 21; *Evening Star,* Aug. 28; *Shipping and Merc. Gazette,* Aug. 20; *Daily News,* Aug. 27; *Times,* Sept. 3; *Star,* Nov. 25; *Manchester Examiner,* Nov. 26; *Leeds Mercury,* Nov. 27, etc.
Against the amendment—
London Standard, Aug. 20; same, Nov. 25; *Globe,* Dec. 22; *Morning Herald,* Aug. 21; same, Sept. 4; *Morning Post,* Aug. 21; same, Aug. 22; same, Aug. 23 (Marcy amendment too favorable to the U. S.); same, Nov. 26; (not practical: England would enlarge her definition of contraband and so continue to capture private property), etc.

[2] See, for the amendment—
Allgemeine Zeitung, May 7, 1856 (Decl. not fair); same, Oct. 21; *Cologne Gazette,* Sept. 3 (but see same, May 11); *L'Assemblée Nationale,* Nov. —; *La Presse Belge,* Sept. 5, 1856 (cannot escape from Marcy's dilemma: allow privateering, or else no capture at all); *Le Constitutionnel,* Dec. 16 (amendment good, but not new); *L'Indépendence Belge,* Aug. 27 (cabinet of Washington justified in looking to its interest) *Le Nord,* June 12, etc.
Against the amendment—
Paris Pays, in *Brussels Le Nord,* Aug. 23 (U. S. selfish); *Paris Siècle,* Aug. 27 (threatens U. S. with coercion), etc.

[3] MS.

to as a device to defeat our negotiations on the 2nd and 3rd principles of the Declaration. It was not necessary that I should more distinctly indicate that than I have done in the replies. In order to put our Ministers abroad in possession of our views *for the purposes of enabling them to prevent as far as possible other Powers from acceding to the Declaration,* * * * I shall send copies of the document to them * * * ." These efforts, apparently, bore but little fruit. In Brazil's notification of accession, March 18, 1858, Sr. Da Silva Paranhos does indeed express his approbation of the amendment; but Brazil accedes nevertheless. On Nov. 24, 1856, Marcy wrote to Dallas that he had received a dispatch from Mr. Mason at Paris declaring that the imperial government would accept the amendment, and adding, "Russia has already done so—and several other powers have received it with favor. If there is sturdy resistance in any quarter it will come from England."[1]

Thus matters stood when the Pierce cabinet retired in March, 1857. In mercantile and shipping circles Marcy was hailed as the champion of humanity and progress; a splendid dinner was tendered to him by the prominent merchants of Baltimore,[2] and the members of the New York Chamber of Commerce, as individuals, united in a petition to President-elect Buchanan to retain him in office.[3] Buchanan, however, observed the danger to the United States that lurked in the proposed amendment perhaps more clearly than its philanthropic author, and caused the British Government to be notified that the United States would be pleased to consider the negotiations suspended. The friends of Marcy, comparing the attitude of the President with his utterances

---

[1] Marcy to Dallas, MS.
[2] *Baltimore Sun*, March 29, 1857.
[3] *Troy Budget*, Feb. 7, 1857.

while ambassador at the Court of St. James,[1] declared that he was simply about to propose an amendment to the amendment, abolishing commercial blockades;[2] but unfortunately, he never did, and the United States remained outside the pale of the Declaration at the outbreak of the Civil War.

[1] "The time will arrive," Mr. Buchanan had then said, "when war against private property on the ocean will be entirely proscribed by all civilized nations, as it has already been upon land." See W. M. Addison, " Ought Private Vessels to be Exempt from Capture in Time of War? The Negative Maintained" (Baltimore, 1856).

[2] *Cf.* the *Boston Traveller*, Aug. 5, 1857; and the *N. Y. Journal of Commerce*, July 31, 1857.

CHAPTER II

THE WORKING OF THE DECLARATION

A PRIORI the Declaration of Paris seems to have, on its practical side, three weak points.

The first is the vagueness of the term "privateering" (*la course*). Marcy, in his letter to Sartiges, predicted that this would infallibly lead to more "unfortunate controversies" than the Declaration assumed to end. Weak maritime states, he declared, would evade the first article by pretending to clothe with a *public* character the vessels of their merchant marine, and privateering would simply be carried on in the name of the state, although in fact no more subject to central control than formerly. Marcy could not, or would not, see any remedy for this condition of things. "Every nation," said he, "would have an undoubted right to declare what vessels should constitute its navy, and what should be requisite to give them the character of public ships," and from the nation's own decision he did not see that there could be any appeal.

The second weakness is the impossibility of securing the proper observance of the second article in the absence of an authoritative definition of contraband. Under the present practice, what is or is not contraband depends upon the wishes of the belligerents as announced from time to time during the war. Constant opportunity is thus afforded for a strong maritime power, such as England, to continue the encroachments upon neutral rights which the Declaration was intended to check; and, by increasing the number of contraband articles indefinitely, practically to destroy the rule that free ships make free goods.

The third weakness is the impossibility of confining the binding effect of the Declaration to "the Powers which have signed or may accede to it." Of course, there is no difficulty in understanding that in case of war between England and Spain, for example, England would be entitled, in spite of the Declaration, to fit out privateers. But suppose war between England on the one hand and allied France and Spain on the other; if the first power issued letters of mark against Spain, the adventurers bearing them would have no right to interfere with French vessels and yet would be subject to capture by every French man-of-war; so that England would be at a disadvantage after all. The inequality with which the Declaration operates is quite as noticeable with regard to article (2). The United States, for example, is not a party to the Declaration; yet in case of war between two signatory powers the United States would be the party really most benefited by article (2), for both belligerents would entrust a large part of their merchandise to American, as neutral, bottoms where, under the Declaration, they would be safe. It is true that neither belligerent owes any duty, under the Declaration, *to the United States;* but each owes a duty to the other,[1] which the remaining parties to the Declaration would not permit to be violated. Similarly, if war occurred between England and the United States, we might safely entrust our goods to French bottoms, while our adversary could not; except, indeed, for the accidental fact that we

[1] Originally the foes of the Declaration denied this; they said that *as between the belligerents themselves*, the Declaration, like all treaties, was abrogated by the war. This was urged several times quite seriously in the House of Commons. There are, of course, two obvious answers. The Declaration is not, in any correct sense, a treaty (though the first article, at any rate, would have been a much more appropriate subject for a treaty than for a declaration); and if it were, treaties made in contemplation of war always survive.

recognize Free Ships Free Goods aside from any of the doings of the Paris Congress.

In the less than half a century which has elapsed since the Declaration, not a few questions of interpretation have arisen; and what has been, gives us a foretaste of what may be.

When the civil war broke out in the United States, and the government at Richmond announced its intention to issue letters of mark, the greatest consternation was produced in the North. Had the United States acceded to the Declaration of Paris, it was reflected, the Southern States, then certainly part of the Union, would have been bound by it, and we might justly have invoked the assistance of foreign nations to prevent its violation. As it was, the immense commerce of the North was exposed, and there was no way of retaliating on the Southerners by sea. In deference to the popular outcry, Mr. Seward, even at the eleventh hour, offered to accede to the Declaration; with the Marcy amendment, if acceptable; if otherwise, without it.[1] The whole of the correspondence on the subject was conducted in thoroughly diplomatic style, carefully avoiding all direct mention of the question at issue—namely, whether, in case of the accession of the United States, the other signatory powers would lend their assistance to keep the seas clear of Confederate privateers. The interchange of notes convinced Mr. Seward that such assistance would not be given, and the offer was withdrawn. The attitude of England and France was unquestionably a correct one. The President's Proclamation of Blockade (April 19) had practically, though not formally,[2] recognized the existence of a state of war between the North and the South; that is, recognized the belligerency of the Confederates; and as soon as the latter

[1] Circular of April 24, 1861; *Dip. Cor.* (1861), p. 34.
[2] *Cf.* Case of the U. S. at Geneva, p. 25.

became belligerents, the power of the Washington government to sign away their belligerent rights fell to the ground. It is, perhaps, fortunate that Mr. Seward's offer was not accepted; if it had been, we should have been bound to the Declaration to-day, and very little of the injury inflicted upon our commerce would have been prevented. As it was, the Alabama was not a "privateer," for Captain Semmes held a commission in the "Confederate navy."[1]

The next case that occurred involving the Declaration was a still simpler one. In 1865 it was agreed, as a matter of course, that Chili, although a party to the Declaration, might commission privateers against Spain, which was not.[2]

In the Franco-German war several interesting questions arose. The King of Prussia, on July 18, 1870, issued a famous decree, announcing that the Prussian navy would not make war upon French merchant vessels.[3] Both Prussia and France had, for a long time, favored the abolition of the capture of private property at sea, and the former, unable to protect her commerce, thought this as good an occasion as any to begin. The attitude of Prussia was warmly commended by the United States, particularly because she had made no condition with regard to reciprocity,[4] but France unfortunately lost her philanthropy at the critical moment, and contented herself with observing the Declaration of Paris; and later the Prussian decree was repealed.

The advantages enjoyed by non-signatory powers like the United States, with large potential carrying trades, became apparent when France announced that although the United States and Spain had not signed the Declaration, they were

[1] *Cf.* Semmes, *Cruise of the Alabama and Sumter* (New York, 1864), p. 106.
[2] Mr. Thompson to Earl Russell, Sept. 30, 1865, enclosing Chilian instructions to privateers, Sept. 26, 1865. *Br. and For. State Papers*, vol. 5, p. 750.
[3] *British and For. St. Papers*, vol. 60, p. 923.
[4] Fish to Baron Gerolt, July 22, 1870, *Br. and For. St. P.*, vol. 61, p. 677.

not to be excepted from the provisions of Article (2).[1] This, as has been shown, was a necessary consequence of the Declaration itself; any other attitude on the part of the French government would have given just ground for offense to Prussia. Thus, one of the three weaknesses became apparent. The disputes as to the right of the Germans to treat coal as contraband, which fill the British and Foreign State Papers relating to this period, showed, in some slight degree, how serious the second weakness might become, especially if England were to uphold the belligerent right against Germany, instead of Germany against England. From our point of view, however, the most interesting dispute was that which arose upon the meaning of the word "Privateering."

On July 23, 1870, the Prussian government notified that of Great Britain that the Declaration of Paris was considered valid and to be observed "throughout the whole of the States of the North German Confederation."[2] On the very next day (July 24), the King, acting under the advice of the Chancellor, issued a decree purporting to provide for the establishment of a volunteer navy. All German seamen and ship-owners were called upon to place themselves at the service of the fatherland. The vessels were to be hired by the state, and one-tenth of their value paid to the owners as deposit; in case of loss, the other nine-tenths was to be paid; in case of restoration, the one-tenth paid was to be reckoned as hire. *The owner was to hire a crew*, the crews were to enter the Federal navy for the war, wear its uniform and badge of rank, take oath to the articles of war, receive pensions at the regular standard, and, if desired, obtain per-

---

[1] *Journal Officiel*, July 25, 1870; Berthémy to Fish, Aug. 3, 1870, *U. S. For. Rel.* (1870), p. 136. See, similarly, the Russian decree of the $\frac{18}{30}$th May, 1877, and the Turkish decision of the 1st of May, 1877. *Br. and For. St. P.*, vol. 68, pp. 921, 924.

[2] Bismarck to Loftus, *Br. and For. St. P.*, vol. 60, p. 924.

manent establishment in the navy as a reward for extraordinary service. The hired ships were to sail under the Federal flag, and to be armed and fitted out at public charge. Premiums from 50,000 thalers down were to be paid to such ships as should capture or destroy ships of the enemy; *and these premiums were to be paid to the owners of the ships, to whom was to be confided the distribution in proper proportions amongst the crew.*[1]

But for the provisions italicised, it would seem impossible to regard the proposed navy as an evasion of the Declaration of Paris. Those two provisions were certainly unfortunate. In its essence, and as it was doubtless honestly intended by the Prussian Government, the scheme was simply for the state to obtain ships for hire, and to increase its navy to a war footing by offering bounties to volunteers. The provision that the volunteers were to be procured by, and the bounties to pass through the hands of, the owners of the ships, who were mere contractors, who had nothing to do with the navy, and who ought to have been allowed, after surrendering their ships and receiving their hire, to drop out of the transaction altogether, was a most unwise and dangerous one, and lent an absurd appearance of private enterprise to a scheme which in its essence was nothing of the sort. The French government saw only the appearance, and protested. England was asked to intervene,[2] and this fact would have shown Mr. Marcy, had he lived to see it, that since the Declaration of Paris every nation has *not* a right to declare what vessels shall constitute its navy; but the Law Officers of the Crown, to whom the matter was submitted by Lord Granville, were of opinion that there were "substantial distinctions" between vessels of the kind proposed and privateers, and Granville, in a polite note to the

---

[1] *British and For. St. P.*, vol. 61, p. 692.
[2] De Lavelette to Granville, Aug. 20, 1870, *ibid.*

French government,[1] declined to do anything more than admonish Prussia not to allow the distinction to fade. As a matter of fact, no Prussian volunteer navy was ever formed, but if it had been, no reasonable construction of the Declaration of Paris would have been violated. At most, the Prussian Government was too economical in employing the same persons as purveyors of ships and recruiting agents; but the vessels hired could not have been privateers for quite a number of reasons: (1) they were actually, by virtue of the contract of hiring, public vessels for the time being, fitted and armed and sent forth at the public expense; (2) their crews were actually public servants, having no right to cruise anywhere except under orders, and subject to the same discipline as the regular navy; and (3) they were designed for the work of a regular navy, and forbidden in fact to prey on private property at all. Under these circumstances the abuses which the first article of the Declaration sought to prevent, would have been quite impossible. But the action of Prussia confirms Mr. Marcy's prediction as to the use which weak maritime states, in the wars of the future, will make of their merchant marines, and gives us an idea just how much of privateering is, and remains, abolished.

The Declaration of Paris is truly, as Mr. Marcy said, a half-way measure. It is inchoate, unfinished, and, it cannot be denied, somewhat faulty, as the first steps of all great reforms have been. But to call it an epoch-making event, or a red-letter day in the calendar of the Law of Nations, would be superfluous. Perhaps that which is to come—the abolition of all capture of private property at sea, including the abolition of commercial blockades—is easier than that which has already been accomplished. In International Law, as in other things, it is the first step that costs. But in honoring

[1] Granville to Lavelette, Aug. 24, 1870. *Br. and For. St. P.*, vol. 61, p. 694.

Walewski and Bourqueney, Buol and Hübner, Clarendon and Cowley, Orloff and Brunnow, Cavour and Villamarina, Manteuffel and Hatzfeldt, Aali-Pacha and Mehemmed-Djemil-Bey, as men well abreast of their time, it will always be a pleasure for Americans to remember our own Secretary of State, who was—we do not know yet how many—years ahead of it.

BIBLIOGRAPHY.

Adams, John. Works. Boston, 1850–1856.
Adams, Henry. History of the United States. N. Y., 1889–1893.
Addison, W. M. Ought Private Vessels to be Exempt from Capture in Time of War? Baltimore, 1856.
Aegidi & Klauhold. Frei Schiff unter Feindes Flagge. Hamburg, 1866.
A General Collection of Treatys and Other Publick Papers (London, 1732).
American and English Encyclopædia of Law.
American Instructions for the Government of Armies in the Field.
American Social Science Association Journal.
American State Papers, Foreign Relations.
American State Papers, Naval Affairs.
Annual Register. (Dodsley's.)
Anquetil. Motifs des Guerres. Paris, an VI.
Azuni. Sistema Universale dei Principii del Diritto Maritimo dell 'Europa. Triest, 1797.
Bancroft. History of the U. S. N. Y., 1884.
Bello. Principios de Derecho Internacional. Caracas, 1847.
Bergbohm. Die Bewaffnete Neutralität. Dorpat, 1883.
Bluntschli. Das Moderne Völkerrecht. Nördlingen, 1878.
Bouvier's Law Dictionary. Boston, 1880.
British & Foreign State Papers.
Bynkershoek. Quaestiones Juris Publici. Lug. Bat., 1751.
Calvo. Droit International. Paris, 1880.
Case of the U. S. at Geneva.
Cauchy. Du Respect de la Propriété Privée. Paris, 1862.
Century Dictionary.
Chateaubriand. Études Historiques. Paris, 1852.
Code of the Institute for Wars on Land.
Coggeshall. History of American Privateers. N. Y., 1856.
Coke. Institutes.
Cooper. History of the Navy of the U. S. N. Y., 1856.
Crowe. History of France. London, 1858–1868.
De Burgh. Maritime International Law. London, 1868.
Diplomatic Correspondence of the U. S.
Doneaud. Histoire de la Marine Française. 3d ed. Paris, n. d.
Emmons. Statistical History of the Navy of the U. S. Washington, 1853.
Fauchille. La Diplomatie Française et la Ligue des Neutres de 1780. Paris, 1893.

Ferguson. Manual of International Law for the Use of Navies and Consulates. The Hague, 1884.
Field. Draft Outlines of an International Code. N. Y., 1872.
Fiore. Nouveau Droit International Public. Paris, 1885.
Force. American Archives. Washington, 1837-51.
Foreign Relations of the U. S.
Franklin. Works. Boston, 1844-1848.
Frothingham. Rise of the Republic of the U. S. Boston, 1881.
Grotius. De Jure Belli ac Pacis. Cambridge, 1853.
Guérin. Histoire Maritime de France. Paris, 1851.
Guernsey. New York City during the War of 1812. N. Y., 1889.
Guizot. Histoire de France depuis 1789. Paris, 1879-80.
Hakluyt. Voyages and Discoveries of the English Nation. London, 1600.
Hall. International Law. Oxford, 1880.
Hautefeuille. Propriétés Privées des Sujets Belligérants sur Mer.
Heffter. Das Europäische Völkerrecht. Berlin, 1873.
Hervey's Naval History of England. London, 1779.
Hildreth's History of the U. S. N. Y., 1849.
Ingersoll. Second War with Great Britain. Phil., 1845.
Ingersoll. War of 1812. Second Series. Phil., 1852.
Jacobsen. Seerecht der Engländer und Franzosen. Hamburg, 1803.
James. Naval History of England. London, 1847.
Jameson. Dictionary of U. S. History. Boston, 1894.
Jefferson. Writings. London, 1829.
Johnson's Encyclopædia.
Journals of Congress.
Kent's Commentaries. London, 1866.
Klüber. Europäisches Völkerrecht. Schaffhausen, 1851.
Lamb and Harrison. History of New York City. N. Y., 1877-1896.
Larousse. Grand Dictionnaire Universel du XIXme Siècle. Paris, 1872.
Laveleye. Du Respect de la Propriété Privée sur Mer en Temps de Guerre. Rev. de Droit Int., 1875.
Lavisse and Rambaud. Histoire Générale du IVme Siècle à Nos Jours. Paris, 1896.
Laws of New York.
Lebeau. Nouveau Code des Prises. Paris, an VII.
Leeder. Die Englische Kaperei und die Thätigkeit der Admiralitätsgerichte. Berlin, 1881.
Littré. Dictionnaire de la Langue Française. Paris, 1873.
Loir. La Marine Française. Paris, 1893.
Lossing's Field-Book of the Revolution. N. Y., 1852.
Lossing's War of 1812. N. Y., 1869.
Lushington. Manual of Naval Prize Law. London, 1866.
Mably. Droit Public de l'Europe fondé sur les Traités. Geneva, 1776.
Maclay. History of the Navy. N. Y., 1894.

McMaster. History of the People of the U. S. N. Y., 1892.
Moniteur.
Napier. History of the Peninsular War. Phil., 1842.
Napoleon. Mémoires. Paris, 1823-5.
Nicolas. History of the Royal Navy. London, 1847.
Niles. American Revolution. Baltimore, 1822.
Nys. La Guerre Maritime. Brussels, 1881.
Ortolan. Règles Internationales et Diplomatie de la Mer. Paris, 1864.
Pardessus. Collection des Lois Maritimes. Paris, 1837.
Phillimore. Commentaries on International Law. London, 1871.
Pierantoni. Rapport sur les Prises Maritimes. Rev. de Droit Int., 1875.
Return of the Names and Number of Russian Vessels Captured, etc., ordered by the House of Commons to be printed, July 29, 1856.
Revue de Droit International.
Riquelme. Elementos de Derecho Público Internacional. Madrid, 1849.
Robinson. Collectanea Maritima. London, 1801.
Rousseau. Du Contrat Social. Paris, 1896.
Schouler. History of the U. S. Washington, 1886.
Secret Journals of Congress.
Select Pleas in the Court of Admiralty (Publications of the Selden Society, Vol. 6 for 1892).
Semmes. Cruise of the Alabama and Sumter. N. Y., 1864.
Sheffield. Privateersmen of Newport. Newport, 1883.
Southey. Lives of the Admirals. London, 1833-40.
Sparks. Diplomatic Correspondence of the American Revolution. Boston, 1829-1830.
Sue. Histoire de la Marine Française. Paris, 1845.
Testa. Droit Public International Maritime. Paris, 1886.
Treaties and Conventions between the U. S. and other Powers. Washington, 1889.
Twiss. Law of Nations in Time of War. London, 1863.
U. S. Statutes at Large.
Vattel. Droit des Gens. Paris, 1830.
Vergé. Notes to Martens. Paris, 1858-1864.
Vidari. Del rispetto della proprietà privata fra gli Stati in guerra. Pavia, 1867.
Webster's Dictionary.
Wharton's Digest of International Law. Washington, 1886.
Wharton's Diplomatic Correspondence of the American Revolution. Washington, 1889.
Wheaton. Elements of International Law. (Dana's ed.) Boston, 1866.
Wheaton. History of the Law of Nations. N. Y., 1845.
Winsor. Narrative and Critical History of America. Cambridge, 1888.
Wolf. Jus Gentium. Magdeburg, 1749.
Woolsey. Introduction to the Study of International Law. N. Y., 1864.

www.ingramcontent.com/pod-product-compliance
Lightning Source LLC
Chambersburg PA
CBHW020830190426
43197CB00037B/1087